Isolde's Way

Isolde McCullagh

Best wishes
Isolde

Ross Print Services

First published 2004 by

Ross Print Services

Greystones, Co. Wicklow, Ireland.

First edition.

A catalogue record for this book is available from the British Library.

ISBN 0-9547653-0-3

Front cover picture:
"Ballet Rehearsal" by Maurice Canning Wilks ARHA RUA (1910-1984)

Dedicated to
my children, Gillian, Dallas and Vanessa,
my grandchildren, Sarah, Kenneth, Hazel, Adam,
David and Mathew
and my great grandson, Paul.

My special thanks to my daughter Gillian
for all her help and encouragement.

Profits from the sale of this book will be donated to the
Blackrock Hospice, Sweetman's Avenue, Blackrock, Co. Dublin.

Family Tree

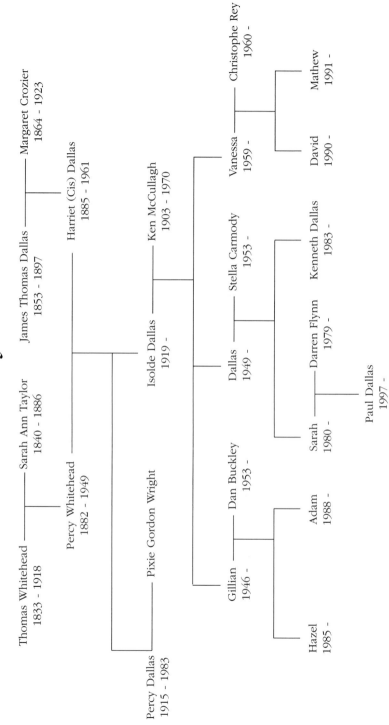

Thomas Whitehead
1833 - 1918

Sarah Ann Taylor
1840 - 1886

James Thomas Dallas
1853 - 1897

Margaret Crozier
1864 - 1923

Percy Whitehead
1882 - 1949

Harriet (Cis) Dallas
1885 - 1961

Pixie Gordon Wright

Isolde Dallas
1919 -

Ken McCullagh
1903 - 1970

Percy Dallas
1915 - 1983

Gillian
1946 -

Dan Buckley
1953 -

Dallas
1949 -

Stella Carmody
1953 -

Vanessa
1959 -

Christophe Rey
1960 -

Hazel
1985 -

Adam
1988 -

Sarah
1980 -

Darren Flynn
1979 -

Kenneth Dallas
1983 -

David
1990 -

Mathew
1991 -

Paul Dallas
1997 -

Foreword

It is more than thirty years since I became associated with the League of Health. My involvement with the League has had a very significant influence on me - both physically and mentally, and is a very important part of my life.

The greatest reward of joining the League was my meeting with Isolde McCullagh. She is a very special person and the living embodiment of our slogan - 'Movement is Life'. To be in her company is a joy. Her classes are filled with vigour and vitality and instilled with her enthusiasm for exercise and a feeling of well being.

Now in her mid-eighties, she is as vital and feisty as when I first met her. She has led and taught the League of Health for 65 years and never lost her enthusiasm. She is surely the living example of 'mens sana in corpore sano'. (A healthy mind in a healthy body)

Speaking for myself, she has enriched my life in many ways. In my professional career as a singer and harpist the League work helped enormously with my breathing and posture.

Isolde has shared her zest for living and her philosophy of a healthy lifestyle with her many thousands of pupils.

I have always felt privileged to know her. Thank you Isolde.

Deirdre O'Callaghan
Patron
The League of Health

February 2004

Photographed on
Kaiteriteri beach, Abel Tasman Bay, South Island, New Zealand.

Isolde McCullagh

Principal: The League of Health Ireland and Extend Ireland

Vice President: The Fitness League UK
                (formerly Women's League of Health & Beauty)

Patron: The Fitness League New Zealand
                (formerly Health & Beauty Exercise N.Z.)

New Zealand
January 2004

I have just achieved one of my long time ambitions, even though I have had to wait until my 85th year to do it – to fly in a hot air balloon.

I arrived in New Zealand five days ago having travelled for some thirty hours to reach the other side of the world. I was met by my daughter Vanessa, who, in turn came from New Caledonia with her two sons David and Mathew, so that we could have five weeks holiday together.

We were collected this morning at 0445 for our Hot Air Balloon adventure and driven to where the balloons are launched. This is a very precise procedure, all are expected to help and safety is a priority at all times. First we had to pile into this oversized "bread basket" to be shown how to hang on. I still haven't accepted the fact nor have my family, that I might find operations such as this slightly more difficult than people half my age! Anyway I managed with the odd shove!

When we were shown exactly how to do this we all had to get out again until the balloon was fully inflated. At this stage both balloon and basket were lying sideways on the ground. I was allowed to get in while the basket was on its side so reached a perpendicular position as the balloon became airborn. After all that the twenty one other passengers from various parts of the world joined me together with the English pilot. From then on it was plain sailing and we reached three and a half thousand feet by the time dawn broke. A truly wonderful sight and a magnificent way to view New Zealand.

Our descent was even more exciting especially as our pilot kept up a stream of comments as to what could happen! We landed in a farmer's field, apparently very few farmers mind this so long as their animals are not in danger. As the passage of the balloon is entirely dependent on the direction of the wind and the pilot's expertise, the final destination is uncertain and to add to the excitement we appeared to miss large areas of trees by inches. There were three balloons airborn and all landed in different fields. Altogether a great experience and I am lucky to have had the opportunity to enjoy it.

Now that I am back to earth again and on holiday, I feel the time has come to put pen to paper. I have had a very varied life and feel privileged to have lived through such a changing world. It has not always been easy but it has made me what I am today and as you will see I still try to live life to the full.

When moving from our family home where we had lived for nearly half a century I found many photos, letters, press cuttings and memories which inspired me to preserve them for the future. Now that I have more time I have decided to write it all down – hence this book.

Contents

Isolde in Invergarry

Early Years

I was born in Dublin in 1919, the younger of two children, my brother Dallas being 4 years and 4 months older. My father, Percy Whitehead was a singer, but he also worked in the Post Office. After the Treaty in 1922 he left the Post Office with a very small pension to concentrate full time on his singing, both performing and teaching.

My mother, Harriet Dallas (Cis), was one of six children, five of them brothers; her father was a Scot and her mother from Northern Ireland. Her father was involved in a boating accident and though not drowned he never fully recovered, her mother was widowed at an early age. I gather she was a real tomboy and very good at sports, even playing mixed hockey.

My mother in her teens

Her brothers Alfie, Ernie and Willie served in the armed forces during the First World War. Willie, the youngest, was in the flying corps and was killed in a flying accident about a month after the Armistice in December 1918. Alfie and Ernie remained in England. The other two brothers, Clairie and Victor, stayed in Dublin to run the family tailoring business, Dallas & Sons in Andrew Street. As the only girl she was very close to her brothers, especially Alfie and Victor, who didn't marry till late in life; as a result they were very special to me.

My mother with Golf Victory Cup

My mother and my father (early portraits)

My mother was engaged to my father for four years before marrying and it was a further four years before my brother was born. In an age when most girls married and had their family very young she would have fitted more easily into the present day. She was a competent, independent woman. She loved her tennis and especially golf, at which she won many trophies.

I remember her as the 'down to earth' parent and my father as the artistic one. Considering this was the very early twentieth century she was very modern in her outlook.

My grandfather, Thomas Whitehead

My father was born in 1882 in Lancashire to Thomas and Sarah Ann Whitehead, he was the youngest of a large family, some of whom died very young. His eldest brother was 21 and had already left for Australia, so he never knew him. His mother died when he was four, so two sisters reared him, Annie in England until he was ten and then Mellie in Dublin, otherwise almost all of his relations still lived in England. He was singing duets with his sister at the age of five. To my knowledge he never had any formal training but was a natural musician to his fingertips. He always played the piano when teaching and could sight-read any music.

MARRIAGE Solemnized in the Parish Church of St. Matthew's Parish, in MANCHESTER, in the County of LANCASTER, in the year 1859

Thomas Whitehead
Sarah Ann Taylor
} of this Parish, were

Married in this Church, on the   6ᵗ   day of November   in the year One Thousand Eight Hundred and Fifty-nine   By   George Airey,
Curate of St: Matthew's.

No. 27b
in the presence of { Thomas Cowin Wilkinson
Ann Ogden

This is an extract taken from the Register of St. MATTHEW'S PARISH CHURCH, in Manchester aforesaid, this   6ᵗ   day of November   1859

George Airey
(Curate)

My grandparent's marriage certificate

My father when young

With my brother

My father had become very well known in the musical world long before I was born or old enough to be aware of his many talents. He won the first of many gold medals and trophies in the Feis Ceoil in Dublin, in 1903 and made his first records in 1912.

When I was about nine years old I became aware that he had a special talent. He had sung as a soloist for twenty-five years with the Culwick Choral Society. To celebrate this occasion they gave a concert in his honour and presented him with a lovely music cabinet, which is now one of my prized possessions.

The audience gave him a great reception but I was not allowed to clap, it obviously wasn't considered correct to applaud one's own family. I am not sure if this was normal or just my mother's inclination to hide one's feelings. I do remember her being cross with my father if she heard him boasting about my brother or me.

The following are caricatures of my father drawn in 1909

"Conquering the World!"

A play on "Percy"

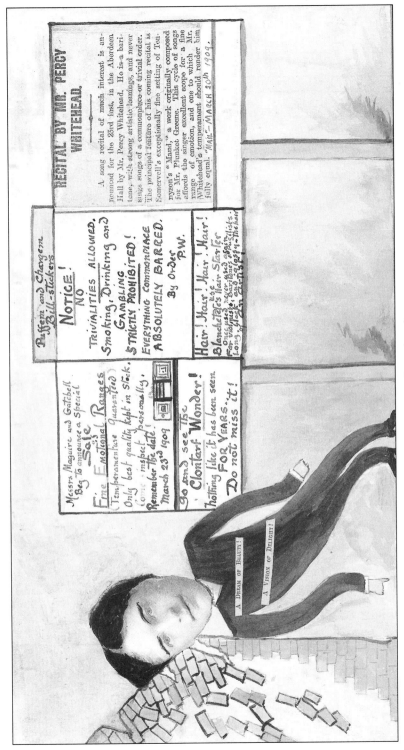

Artistic Leanings!

The following are some newspaper cuttings about my father

DUBLIN'S NEW BARITONE,
MR. PERCY WHITEHEAD,

Whose singing gave so much pleasure after
the recent State Dinner in Dublin Castle,
and whose very interesting song recital will
take place next Tuesday evening.

Mr. Percy Whitehead, who had the honour of singing after the recent State Dinner in Dublin Castle, and whose Song-Recital on next Tuesday evening in the Gresham Hotel promises to be so successful, both from a social and musical point of view, is one of our most charming as well as our youngest Dublin singers.

* * *

A year ago the greatest fault which could be found with Mr. Whitehead was that his very fine voice was not sufficiently well known in Dublin.

* * *

Slowly but very surely he has been overcoming this objection, and to-day is well advanced on the way to a speedy and well-deserved success, with a strongly-increasing host of friends and admirers.

* * *

Mr. Whitehead started his musical career by obtaining a gold medal in the Feis of 1903—the same year that McCormack won the medal in tenor competition.

* * *

And it may be an omen of Mr. White-head's future career that he was so associated at its outset with that famous artist.

* * *

Mr. Whitehead's temperament enables him to do full justice to emotional and dramatic music, and the Somervell setting of "Maud," which is being made a special feature of the concert on the 23rd, forms a series of beautiful tone-pictures when interpreted by him.

Newspaper Cutting - Irish Society 20/3/1909

10

THE MAIL,

MARCH 24, 1909.

MR. PERCY WHITEHEAD'S SONG RECITAL

Attracted by the announcement of Mr. Percy Whitehead's Song Recital, there was a large attendance last night at the Aberdeen Hall, Gresham Hotel. The audience was chiefly composed of that section of fashionable Dublin devoted to music from tradition and taste. Of his many musical friends Mr. Whitehead, with much judgment, selected only three to assist him, Mr. Clyde Twelvetrees, Miss Nettie Edwards, and Mr. C. W. Wilson. Thus while remaining, with the fullest accord of his admirers, the central figure of the evening, this circumstance gave much additional interest to the occasion.

Desirous of not sparing himself, the better to satisfy his audience of his undoubted versatility, Mr. Whitehead selected eight songs by various composers, and of widely differing periods, giving as well Somervell's beautiful, but lengthy, song-cycle "Maud."

Mr. Whitehead has a fine baritone voice. He has a pleasing manner. He makes no attempt to be dramatic in his movements, relying chiefly on his voice, full of the capacity for feeling, to make his meaning clear. But the varying expressions of his face, alive with character, are more convincing than most dramatic movements. The quietness and ease with which he sings are indeed qualities to be proud of. Naturally the songs selected were those best suited to the capabilities of the singer, and so he proceeded from song to song with perfect assurance, as if certain of the success, following success, with which he met. In the song-cycle he rose admirably to its exhausting requirements, due to its length, without losing the interest of his hearers for a moment. It was a fine test, and the result was most satisfying. Of the other songs, all were so finished in rendering, both grave and gay, tender and forceful, that it is difficult to make a selection. On the whole, the Schumann setting of Moore's exquisite song, "Row gently here," was as perfectly sung as any. Thoroughly delighted with his singing, the large audience loudly applauded Mr. Whitehead on each succeeding appearance, insisting at the end on an encore, which was generously responded to. A handsome laurel trophy, bearing the inscription, "Maud," in gilt letters, was presented to him at the conclusion of the song-cycle. The book of words supplied was most welcome, but the singer's clear enunciation made it almost unnecessary. It was so daintily printed, however, that it was quite a worthy souvenir of a most memorable occasion.

Besides several 'cello solos, Mr. Clyde Twelvetrees took part in "Variations" (Mendelssohn), a duet for piano and 'cello, with Mr. C. W. Wilson, who played the accompaniments of the evening. Miss Nettie Edwards sang numbers from "Fidelio," and later on "Elsa's Dream."

C. A.

Newspaper Cutting - The Mail 24/3/1909

The Irish Times.

MONDAY, NOVEMBER 14, 1910.

concerts. Mr. Percy Whitehead was the vocalist, and in "O God, have mercy," from Mendelssohn's "St. Paul," and songs by Cornelius and Strauss, exhibited his usual gifts of temperament, and also artistic finish.

The Freeman's Journal
→ AND →
National Press

DUBLIN: MONDAY, NOVEMBER 14, 1910.

Mr. Percy Whithead, possessing a robust baritone voice, sang effectively "O God, Have Mercy" (Mendelssohn), and "The Kings" (Cornelius), and "Zueignung" (R. Strauss). He was loudly and deservedly recalled.

DUBLIN, MONDAY, NOV. 14, 1910.

Mr. Whitehead sang three songs, Mendelssohn's "O God, Have Mercy," and two bracketed items, "The Kings" and "Zueignung." His first song was perhaps his best, his rendering showing artistic appreciation of the essentially religious spirit of the aria, but all were beautifully sung.

Dublin
Evening Mail
ESTABLISHED 1823.

DUBLIN, MONDAY, NOV. 14, 1910.

forms. Mr. Percy Whitehead was much at home in his rendering of "O, God have Mercy," from Mendelsshon's "St. Paul," and other numbers, his fine voice being admirably suited in each case.

Newspaper cuttings concerning
Sunday Orchestral Concert - 13/11/1910

Mr. Percy Whitehead contributed many songs and encores. He is one of our finest singers in that he has no irritating mannerisms suggestive of voice production. His songs from Schumann were all through full of tenderness and charm, his old English "Self-banished" (Dr. Blow) at times intense in feeling, and the "Roadside Fire" (Vaughan Williams), and "The Devon Maid" (Hamilton Harty), two highly-coloured episodes of abandonment to nature and exceedingly "simple life."

Newspaper Cutting - The Irish Times 24/11/13

THE CULWICK CHORAL SOCIETY.

MR. PERCY WHITEHEAD'S 25th ANNIVERSARY.

The choir generously made it a Whitehead night. It is twenty-five years since Mr. Percy Whitehead won the gold medal in his class at the Feis Ceoil, and was invited by Dr. Culwick to sing at a concert of the Orpheus Society in the following November. The seriousness with which Mr. Whitehead always has treated his art was illustrated last night by his introducing to a Dublin audience a set of the interesting and difficult songs of Peter Warlock, one of the most adventurous song-writers of to-day. There still is no singer in Dublin who could deliver such songs as convincingly as Mr. Whitehead. Besides the solos in the "Cavalier Songs" of Stanford, he sang a charming set of five Christmas

songs (including that "O Jesulein Süss" hymn which Bach harmonised so beautifully for choir-singing); but his breaking of new ground in the Warlock songs at this stage in his career was his triumph last night. In them he found excellent scope for his special gift of humorous—but still artistic—delivery. The "Roister Doister" was as good a bit of work in that vein as ever he has done.

Mr. Whitehead himself led the tribute to Miss Dorothy Stokes's skill in accompaniment, which was put to the sternest test in the Warlock songs.

Newspaper Cutting - The Irish Times 23/11/28

In the early 1930s he decided to stop performing and devote all his time to training pupils, though he continued in the Christ Church Cathedral Choir for many years. It was only through my research for this book that I discovered the huge number of recitals he gave and how much he was in demand as a soloist. All this was long before the microphone became an essential tool for most singers. He could sing pianissimo and be heard at the back of the Theatre Royal or indeed at a Promenade Concert conducted by Henry Wood.

People found it very hard to understand that he stopped singing in public when he was at his best, but that is why he did stop; he preferred to be remembered that way and not as an ageing singer, I also think that teaching was his true vocation.

LADIES' CHOIR BROADCASTS

By HAROLD R. WHITE
("Irish Independent" Music Critic.)

A circumstance which to some degree accounts for the musical excellence of the Tudor Ladies' Choir is the ability of the conductor. Percy Whitehead has been for many years associated with vocal music of the highest class, first as a singer, and later as trainer.

One could realise from the broadcast of the Tudor Ladies' Choir that the individual voices were trained, not merely in the important matter of production, but in diction and interpretation as a team.

The purity of the tone in Harrison's "Most Gentle Moon" and Handel's "Sweet Day So Cool" was due largely to the restraint and simplicity of the singing. In Macfarren's dainty "You Spotted Snakes" an attractive feature was the gently insistent rhythm of the "Philomel" figure.

EXPRESSIVE SONG.

One of the most expressive of the songs was Charles Wood's "Music, When Soft Voices Die." The harmonies were exquisitely modulated and the accompaniment blended perfectly with the voices. The delicate staccato in Walker's "Say Dainty Dames" was enjoyable.

The soloist was Molly Dunlop, whose pleasant contralto was adequate in Hughes's "Blue Hills of Antrim" and several other Anglo-Irish songs by Hughes and Peterkin.

Newspaper Cutting - 30/1/41

TUDOR LADIES' CHOIR

LAST NIGHT'S CONCERT

Part singing, well-nigh as perfect as could be, was heard by the Tudor Ladies' Choir at their concert in the Leinster Hall, Royal Hibernian Hotel, Dublin, last night. In this select group Mr. Percy Whitehead, the conductor, has a grand lot of trained voices, with a musical knowledge and vocal control that enables him to give full play to the interpretation of their songs. These singers listen to each other, and so achieve that splendid unity of tone in the respective parts which helps to make their work so pleasing. The parts are artistically balanced, and the chording is always full, the inner voices being especially rich. In their singing last night they achieved beautiful effects in "The Silver Swan" (Orlando Gibbons), "What Saith My Dainty Darling" (T. Morley) and other madrigals. There was a beautiful sense of atmosphere in

their treatment of Henschel's "Out of the Deep," and a dainty finement in Schubert's "The Lord is My Shepherd." But in a lengthy programme there was not a single item that had not its especial feature. It was choral work of the most finished style.

Some excellent songs were contributed by Evelyn Nesbitt and Mary Dempster O'Neill, and very skilled violin playing was heard from Isidore Shlaen. Dorothy Stokes was the accompanist, and better there could not have been.

Newspaper Cutting - 22/1/42

Newspaper Cutting - 1/3/44
Irish Times

During the years 1927 – 29 his pupils won thirty-four gold medals, five silver and four bronze at the Feis Ceoil. Shortly after that he formed the Tudor Ladies Choir, which consisted of his own pupils. They went on to win the Culwick Cup, five years in succession, and also won a similar competition for five years in Belfast. My father then realized that they weren't too popular with the other contestants, so they just performed at their own concerts once a year. He had about twenty-four ladies in the choir, all of them soloists in their own right.

Irish Musicians' Who's Who

Percy Whitehead, in the year 1903, won the Bass Medal, when John McCormack won the Tenor Medal at the Feis Ceoil. Whitehead had a cathedral training and a *flair* for sight-reading.

Denis O'Sullivan was greatly attracted to his style, and gave him much valuable advice. In 1908 the late Harry Plunket Greene presented a cup to the Feis Ceoil for "Interpretation," and Whitehead won it, as well as the Denis O'Sullivan Medal. That was a great day for Whitehead, "H. P. G.," as he calls him affectionately, became—not only a personal friend, but a mentor and teacher, and, to the end of H.P.G.'s career, received from Whitehead the confidence which one artist expects from his brother-artist.

Mr. Percy Whitehead.

Whitehead has given recitals all over England and Wales, and in every musical centre in Ireland, but, peculiarly, he never sang in Cork. Concert appearances have included those with "H.P.G.," John Coates, Rosini Buckman, Carrie Tubb, and heaps of others. In oratorio he has appeared with the Old Dublin Philharmonic, under Dr. Charles Marchant, and in countless church performances. He has a unique record, in that teaching has compelled him to forego performance whilst still a comparatively young man. His reward has been through his pupils, of whom I mention Laelia Finneberg, Robert Irwin, John L. Woods, Frank Cowle and Robert McCullagh.

Percy Whitehead, all through his carreer, has had the genius of co-ordinating two words—"simplicity" and "sincerity." These are perhaps the two finest words not only in art, but in life. He is always at ease on the platform, with a genuine effort to please and to remain an artist, and a sense of humour which carries. But then, that is art, and art's interpretation.

Newspaper Cutting

Dugort

Dugort, Terenure Road

Three years old

Before I was three years old, we had moved to a big old house called 'Dugort' on Terenure Road. From an early age I was brought to my father's concerts and it was a great thrill when I was allowed to help my mother with the floral arrangements. When I was about three I went to dancing school and from then on took part in yearly matinees.

I was always practising and copying the bigger girls' solos, so much so that on one occasion I escaped from the chorus and danced behind a girl whose big day it was. I understand the audience thoroughly enjoyed the performance, but the girl's mother never forgave me! This episode I don't remember but I do recall my first solo at the age of five. I remember the very pretty dress I wore and the fact that the conductor of the orchestra smiled at me. I was so captivated by him that I don't think I did the dance I was taught.

Though I was strictly brought up it was a very happy home. I loved dancing and singing and also was always mimicking people; this trait, together with my sense of humour I think I inherited from my father. Though he might have indulged me, my mother wouldn't let him.

My brother was christened Percy Dallas and I was christened Isolde Dallas. Dallas was my mother's maiden name and now it occurs regularly as a first or second name in the McCullagh male line, so it was familiar to us long before President Kennedy was assassinated or the soap 'Dallas' became popular. I even have a cousin with the surname Dallas and the initials J.R! James Ross (Ross) is a son of my Uncle Clairie. Ross and his sisters, Vivienne and Peg all live in Ireland.

I wrote this letter to my father when I was staying with Uncle Clairie and his family in Sandymount.

Dugort

July 19th 1929.

My dear Daddy

We are glad to hear you had a good passage and arrived safely. I am writing for Mummy as she is trying to get all she can done today so that she will not have much to do to-morrow. Mummy won her match on Wednesday

6-2, 7-5, so she has to play at the "At Home" to-morrow and she also has to bake for it. I had a very nice day at Sandymount. I bathed and played cricket but unfortunately I got a shell in my heel which made a cut over an inch long. Mummy says that she could not allow me out of her sight

without something happening me. Dallas did not go to see your boat going out. He went to Perry's for his bike and on to the tennis. There has been no post for you except the electric light bill. I got my certificate from the Read school and past with first class honours. On the post this

19

excuse writing.
morning I got a postal order
for seven shillings from Auntie
Ria & Auntie Annie. Mammy
is going to buy me a bathing
wrap. Thank Uncle Alfie for the
five shillings he sent me give
him our love and a special
kiss for yourself
Love
from
Soda

I was very young when I started singing and learning voice production from my father and it is this training that has stood to me all my life in the career I finally chose. I belonged to a children's organization attached to a church. We had monthly concerts and yearly competitions for singing, elocution and piano playing. This again was great training for me. I never had any fear of being on a stage in front of an audience, but I am sure I was as nervous as anybody until I got going. Perhaps the greatest lesson I learnt was that the "show must go on", no matter how sick you might be.

I can remember very clearly being brought to the Gaiety Theatre in a taxi, my mother had made a flannel wrap to put round my body, under my tutu, so that I wouldn't get more ill. There was no way I would want to or would be allowed to let anybody down. I can remember feeling sorry for the children whose costumes weren't properly cared for. By this time I was learning from Eveline Burchell, who proved to be the foremost dancing teacher of her time. She was a very hard taskmaster but I loved it all.

Age 12 at Eveline Burchills

DANCING RECITAL

Miss Eveline Burchill needs no introduction to the Dublin public, and the dancing matinee given in the Gaiety Theatre yesterday adds still further laurels to an already distinguished list. All through a long and extraordinarily varied programme the standard exhibited was of the highest. Operatic, acrobatic, and tap were each dealt with in turn in a most accomplished manner.

Miss Eileen Robinson was the star in a very gay firmament. Her technique, as portrayed in "Slow Motion," was splendid. George Begley, as her partner, was also conspicuous, especially in his elevation. Again in the dance, "In a Persian Garden," this couple further distinguished themselves. In this number, Miss Isolde Whitehead as a Fruit Seller, gave a very finished performance. The setting in the dance, "In a Monastery Garden," was very appropriate, and here again, as a statue, Miss Whitehead calls for special notice.

A very pretty and brightly coloured Ballet concluded the first part, and a realistic Eastern scene brought the whole performance to a close.

Miss Burchill is to be congratulated on the fruits of her labours and the success of the matinee

Newspaper Cutting - about 1932-1933

Looking back, I suppose I was bound to end up a teacher as I was always teaching my friends to do the acrobatics that I loved. My parents were really very tolerant as I was rarely to be seen other than upside down. We lived in a big old style house and there was a settee in the hall, which I was allowed to jump on and somersault on and all my friends followed suit.

At 7 years old I had joined the Guide Movement as a Brownie and continued through the movement until I went to London at the age of 19 to train in the League. Looking back I realize that I had a very full and productive childhood, which left little or no time to get into mischief; this is a policy I continued with my own children, to be bored was just not acceptable.

Guides (I am on right, back row)

I was at a private junior school until I was twelve. For my secondary education I went to Alexandra School; on my first day I met two girls, Sheila Polden and Truda Mossop, both of whom have remained lifelong friends. Truda emigrated to Australia some time after the 1939-45 war, but we keep in touch regularly.

Truda and me - Ballymoney

Alexandra College, Dublin

Sheila, like myself is a widow but lives only a few miles away, we meet regularly and she is still a League member. When I was fifteen I damaged the cartilage in my left knee, while performing in the Gaiety. This gave my parents the excuse they wanted to stop my dancing as my schoolwork was suffering. I fought hard over this, but to no avail. They probably had a couple of difficult years with me as I thought my heart was broken.

The greatest treasure the
world can hold
Search as you will, end to end
Is not power, or fame, or
gold,
But just the love of a
friend

from: Truda with love

An example of Truda's artistic ability

At sixteen I went to Alexandra College. In those days the School and College were separate and situated in Earlsfort Terrace. The College was for students who wanted to stay in Secondary Education to do their School Leaving Examinations. It also had Secretarial Training, Froebel and Domestic Science courses at third level. I can't say I really enjoyed school but I loved college, where we were treated as students. We had free periods in which we could do gymnastics, but only once a day. We had lots of apparatus, so I had a wonderful time.

After two years I sat the Senior Cambridge Examination and then went to stay for nine weeks in Bristol with my mother's brother - my Uncle Ernie, his wife Elsie and daughters Maureen and Pat. I joined the local swimming club, their headquarters being a big lake. Though very cold, it had the advantage of not hurting so much when I crashed while practising my dives; the salt water can be very painful on impact.

Bristol - Age 18

Whenever I was away my father used to write me amusing letters and poems. In keeping with his sense of humour, these were written 'tongue in cheek' and should be read as such. This one was sent to me while I was on holiday in Bristol with Uncle Ernie and his family.

25/8/37

My dear little Omelette

> *If I'm an egg, you're a cracked one.*
>
> *I hope the enclosed donation will to some extent, allay the financial drought – from which we all suffer at times. Even I have been known to want money. I stayed in the caravan & read myself nearly to sleep. Then I got fed up & thought I'd go to White Walls for some "bloody" books & I'd hardly put my feet on the wet ground when they went from under me & I simply slid down the hill on my latter end until a tuft of grass arrested my progress. So I went sadly over to Auntie Kathleen & had a good wash in her bathroom & scraped half Ballymoney off my pants. Tell Auntie Ria I don't need to go to Brandon Hill to fall around. I can do it locally!*
>
> *We had Mr. & Mrs W. in for a game last night & when Mammy was heating the coffee over the Primus a certain portion of her anatomy caught the handle of the pan as she was turning & most of the coffee was subsequently used to wash the floor. There's really not room for her to turn in the caravan & from a casual survey I should say she can still give you a few inches round the equator.*
>
> *Glad you are having a good time. When do you expect to return? I think we miss you. Personally I don't get bullied quite so much as when you are around but I think I could put up with you if you were here.*
>
> *Ever your affectionate*
>
> *Daddy*

I was lucky enough to have the West of England diving coach interested in me, which was a great help when I returned to Dublin and trained for the Irish swimming and diving championships. Considering that Blackrock baths was the only place where we could dive, I wonder anyone achieved any sort of standard; standing on the diving boards with a strong East wind blowing was no fun. Now Blackrock and Dun Laoghaire baths are permanently closed and there are no pool facilities whatever for the young people to swim, let alone dive, in the open air during the summer months.

During the winter, we trained in the Iveagh Baths and Tara Street. The latter was not even filtered and of course both were too shallow to allow diving. We accepted this because we had no choice, but it was only the truly dedicated that bothered, especially as most of us had to cycle to and from training, even though we lived some miles away and even in the depths of winter. I received the following letter from my father while on holiday in Sligo.

December 1937

Dugort, Terenure Rd

Dublin

My dear pet Lambikin,

> *I write to let you know that this leaves me in the best of health, & as I'm not going to waste my lovely notepaper and Telephone no: on you, I propose to utilise this ruled paper & carefully keep to the straight and narrow path.*

I can't tell you how we miss you! I toured the long pantry yesterday and I found the butler going bad in its wrappings, bananas rotting on their stalk, biscuits softening in their tins and the curranty bun hardly able to hold up its head. On the other side, expenses have gone down to zero, we've told Colgans we want nothing for a week and Meehan's have given up business. Incidentally I'm sorry for the Blackburns. We never before realised what a burden you were – financially and gastronomically. (Ha! Ha! That has you).

> *I am sure you are having a good time and trying to live up to the good opinion (rightly or wrongly) your Daddy has of you. Even tho' I've written a deal of nonsense (as they say in Lancashire) you may read between the lines that I love you very much and really miss you. I didn't think the house could be so quiet.*

Send me a line if you can spare a minute.

> *With love from us all*

> > *Daddy*

Have you heard of a "little pet lamb"
Who displayed a strong weakness for
hamb

She would mop all she got
Coming hot from the pot,
But if cold – she would just murmur
"Damb"
(Copyright by Sharts & Kelly)
6/1

One of my acrobatic poses!

Childhood Memories

These are written as they came to my mind, rather than in any chronological order.

❑ Going by tram with my mother to visit her mother in Clontarf, who died when I was three. I think I remember her, but possibly only because of seeing photos. I had no other living grandparents.

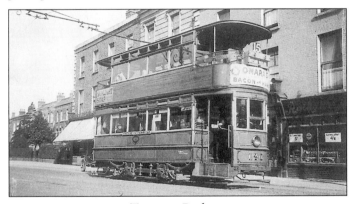

Tram at Rathgar

❑ Watching girls in their communion dresses and veils, wishing I was a Roman Catholic so that I could be dressed like that. There was a Chapel nearby, so I could see the children from an upstairs window.

With Nanny

❑ From the time I was a baby, we had a maid cum nanny whom I adored, she married the local postman. She was still living with us and my mother gave her away. I think I was about 7 years old. I missed her very much, though visited her a lot. Sadly a year later she died in childbirth and I can still remember the loss I felt. I tried to hide this from my parents. I think I have always hidden my worries and sorrows, which is a bad trait and tends to give the impression of not caring.

❑ Another great memory – going to the motor racing practices in the Phoenix Park with my father, which took place very early in the morning. I still have my autograph book with many famous signatures, including those of Malcolm Campbell Senior and Earl Howe. Mountjoy Corner was considered the most dangerous part. Years later my brother tried to emanate their prowess in his little Austin; he turned the car over, but was fortunately thrown clear. Though the cars couldn't travel as fast as nowadays, there were many serious accidents, because the cars were not built so well.

Our family

❑ Going all the way from Terenure to ride on the Hill of Howth tram – a day's outing.

❑ Our first car, a little Clyno IZ 1882, I was only eight or nine but I never forgot the number, probably because my father was born in 1882. Once we were independently mobile, we came to know every inch of the Dublin and Wicklow mountains. My brother and I were always looking for an old ruin we could climb or a river we could ford. Needless to say, with the difference of four years in our ages, I was constantly coming to grief or ending up in a river. My mother used to say that if Dallas asked me to jump into the Liffey, I would probably do it.

❏ We always took an annual trip to Lucan and Poulaphouca in the autumn to see the wonderful colouring of the trees. Of course this was years before Poulaphouca was flooded to make a reservoir. We always had a picnic on these trips.

Our rented cottage in Rush

Doing my best to get wet!

With my father and brother, Dallas

❏	Our summer holiday was a month in Rush, near the sea in north County Dublin; we stayed in a rented cottage.

Our water supply was the village pump and our lighting - paraffin lamps and candles. We always went by taxi, which was a major journey. One year particularly sticks in my mind as our Kerry Blue had had pups, so we were accompanied by her and five pups in the taxi.

I can still see my mother cleaning the cottage from top to bottom before leaving. We all had to be outside when she finally reversed out on her hands and knees, making sure that the floor was spotless. In later years I often thought of this when I rented out our seaside bungalow or a caravan and had to spend hours cleaning up the mess left by the tenants. A sad reflection on how people treat other peoples' property.

❏	My mother was a very good cook and everything was made at home. I learnt so much from her and even now find it hard to understand that most things are bought ready to cook or eat and the present generation never had the opportunity to learn these skills.

❏	Wash day – always on a Monday, my mother with a big zinc bath on the kitchen table, washing all the delicate clothing. On the other side of the table, the maid had the washtub on two chairs and a scrubbing board for sheets, towels, etc. There was a big wringer and everything was carefully folded before being put through in order to make the ironing easier to keep them in shape. There was also a big enamel lined cauldron for boiling the whites. This utensil was also used for boiling the Christmas puddings.

❏	Then another of my memories was practicing my dancing in the kitchen, getting over-enthusiastic, falling on the flagstones and splitting my lip open.

That evening I was appearing in a show representing Robinson's jam, carrying a golliwog. The latter has just recently been removed from their label, as it is considered 'politically incorrect'. I have no idea how or why I was involved but remember it vividly.

❏	Going to sleep at night, directly above where my father was teaching. To this day I am reminded of it, when I hear certain songs, so it was quite easy for me when he started training me. I was probably about eight and sang in my first competition at the age of nine.

Robinson's jam with Golly   *Reading the lesson! - age 3*

❏   By 1931 we had a larger car, so during the summer we took the car to England, travelled through Wales to Tavistock in Devon, where my mother's brother, Uncle Ernie, lived with his family. All together we booked a house in Perranporth, Cornwall. Two years we did this and these holidays stand out as the happiest of my life. My uncle had been a gymnast, so he taught my brother and me all sorts of tumbles.

We also made human pyramids, being the smallest and the lightest, I was always on the top, thus had the furthest to fall! My mother and Auntie Elsie cooked us wonderful meals. I realize now how we took them for granted. I also remember I spent all my pocket money on chocolate; it was during these holidays I learnt to embroider.

Me on top, Uncle Ernie, my brother, my father on bottom
(Perranporth)

❏ In 1934 we had our first caravan holiday. In those days you stayed where you wanted – up a laneway or in a farmer's field or on the edge of a cliff. One of these places was in Roundstone, Connemara, where one night there was a bad storm and I think my parents thought we were going to end up on the rocks or even the sea. My brother and I thought it was very exciting.

Our Citroen with hired caravan

We had Shandy with us but we put her son Crusoe in kennels. Because we were moving around we got a letter to say he had died, before we heard that he was fretting. I was devastated and to this day I can remember our feeling of guilt that we just didn't realize the bond there was between the two of them; the son had never been parted from his mother. We humans have much to learn from animals.

If we were near a farmer it was not unusual to find a can of fresh milk at the door in the morning. A dozen eggs meant thirteen!

One morning we awoke to a strange noise, when we investigated we found a cow chewing the corner of the caravan!

Any time we were near the coast we could buy a lobster for a shilling and the local hotel would cook it for us (no charge).

Quite often we got into difficulties going down a narrow lane and discovering there was nowhere we could turn. My brother was the expert here as he could reverse the car with the caravan attached without ending up in the ditch!

Shandy   *Crusoe*

When we moved from place to place I was detailed off to stay in the caravan for the first mile or so to make sure everything was properly fixed – this was guaranteed to make me feel sick, much worse than a rough sea!

❏   Around about this time I had an Easter holiday with my friend Sheila, whose parents had a section of the old Coastguard station in Ballymoney, Co. Wexford.

I loved this, swimming in the cold sea, then dressing in front of a big range in the kitchen. Lighting was with paraffin lamps and bedtime was with candles. Thus began years of holidaying there, either camping or caravanning and indeed renting one of the houses when I had my own children. Uncle Ernie and family, with whom we had holidayed in Cornwall came to join us in Ballymoney for a holiday twice before the Second World War, once again we had a wonderful time together.

❏   While still in my teens I camped there with my friends, Sheila and Truda; we were on our own and yet perfectly safe.

We had quite a distance to walk to get water but it was all part of the fun. Hard to believe that nowadays. We think of the young of today as having so much freedom but actually we had

Coastguard Station, Ballymoney, Co. Wexford

a much freer and carefree life, without the dangers so prevalent now. A group of us used to walk into Courtown to the Saturday night dance and return via the beach, finishing off with a midnight swim. I look back on those days with great nostalgia. It was on these holidays I discovered my ability as a water diviner.

Truda, me and Sheila - Ballymoney

> To my little Darling.
>
> There once was a lassie named Izzy.
> Who sat in the sun & went dizzy.
> As she fell on her head,
> She smiled faintly & said,
> Bring me "Andrew" — its cool & its fizzy

> To She - Shi.
>
> If you're only twelve stone eight,
> And you want to put on weight.
> Just try a course of Cadbury or Fry.
> Take a slab three times a day,
> Keep starvation far away,
> And you'll look like little Sheila by and bye.

Sent during one of our camping holidays

❏ Rugby matches – Lansdowne Road, every Saturday with my father. I still love watching Rugby, though I must admit I now watch it on television.

❏ Each year my father entered many pupils for the Feis Ceoil. He had in the early days won many competitions himself. The Sunday evening before the start of the Feis my mother always had a supper for all his pupils and they all had to sing, with him accompanying them - a rehearsal, if you like for their performance during the week. I always seemed to be there and dragged into it, to do my own performance, usually doing a backbend, or standing on my hands or cartwheels or whatever, but sometimes I know I did sing. One of his pupils was Laelia Finneberg, she won five competitions in the one year, she was trained solely by my father. Some of his many pupils were Frank Cowle, Bob McCullagh, Robert Irwin, Evelyn Nesbitt and Molly Dunlop.

THE 1928 Feis Ceoil will probably go down in musical history as the Fineberg Feis owing to the remarkable achievements of Miss Laelia Fineberg in carrying off no less than five of the chief honours of the festival. She won the Plunket Greene Cup for song interpretation; the Wallis Cup for singing to her own pianoforte accompaniment; the Denis O'Sullivan Medal for singing of Irish songs; the Gervase Elwes Cup for artistic singing; and the Rathmines Cup for dramatic solo singing and acting in character costume.

Miss Fineberg is not a newcomer to the Feis, but her development during the past year has been quite extraordinary. It is only necessary to read the almost extravagant praise given her by Lady Harty and Mr. Walter Hyde to realise that she is an artiste of rare distinction. She seems to have no nerves, and sings with an assurance and poise that many celebrities might well envy.

The success of this gifted singer may result in a change of the Feis Ceoil rules, as the committee can hardly view with equanimity the possibility of any competitor in the future setting out to break Miss Fineberg's record.

Some years ago when a lady won both the contralto and mezzo-soprano competitions the committee framed a rule confining solo singing entrants to one class of voice only. It may well happen now that unlimited entries will be confined to instrumental competitions where the chance of winning several prizes is restricted by the variety of technique required.

Miss Fineberg has won a distinction of which she and her teachers may well be proud.

Newspaper Cutting - 1928

❑   A friend, Hilda Houston and I were always putting on our own shows and charging '3d' for admission, which we gave to charity, even then I must have had the desire to be a producer and a business woman! We called ourselves 'Castor and Pollux'.

❑   My birthdays, - I am lucky enough to have a birthday in June. I look back and think of them always as sunny days. I was allowed to have a couple of friends to tea and we picnicked in the garden, much enjoying the special treats produced by my mother.

Perhaps the weather was no different from what we can expect today, but my memory is beautiful sunny days and picnicking on the grass in our back garden.

Dugort - Birthday Picnic Tea

❏ Standing on top of the dunes in Portnoo, Co. Donegal, my father and I admiring the view and chatting. Suddenly I realised I was on my own. Looking down I saw him lying flat on his back, laughing away; of course I was convulsed with laughter also, once I saw he wasn't hurt. All the same it was a salutary lesson to us both to stand well back from any precipice.

❏ That caravan holiday is particularly vivid to me as I was able to practice my firm stage diving from the pier and also that my father drove me back to Dublin for a diving competition. It seemed an endless journey and quite an undertaking back in the 1930s. This was yet another example of how my parents took so much interest and gave me so much support in all my activities. At the same time I learnt to be independent at an early age.

❏ My father was one of the first to broadcast from London, then known as Droitwich and from Dublin, which was known as 2RN in those days. We had a little crystal set; having put on our ear-phones, we could tune in by adjusting the 'cat's whisker', this was a very fine wire and we would put it on the crystal until we could hear his voice, a very delicate operation and very frustrating. Of course we could listen to him on our wind-up gramophone as he made his first records in 1912, spending the proceeds on buying his piano, which is still a treasured family possession.

I still have some of my father's records, handmade, voice on one side only and of course 78 r.p.m. speed. I remember seeing a loudspeaker for the first time in a friend's house, it was exactly like the picture on 'His Master's Voice' and very harsh in tone.

Newspaper Cutting - The Irish Times 8/2/12

Mr. PERCY WHITEHEAD.

Ireland's Greatest Baritone.

10-inch Records, 3s. 6d.

G.C. 4-2191   **I know where I'm going**   *arr. by Hughes*

Percy Whitehead.

MR. WHITEHEAD is a baritone singer new to our catalogue, who is likely to make his mark wherever his voice is heard. He possesses a unique gift of reproducing emotion, and this is exemplified by the haunting pathos which he imparts to this old ballad. The dying away effects of the concluding lines,

> " I know who I love,
>   But the dear knows
>   who I'll marry,"

marks him at once as a rare and finished artist, and the song gives unique and beautiful expression to the emotion of love. (*Speed* 81.)

Published by Boosey & Co.

G.C. 4-2192   **Johneen**   *Stanford*

JOHNEEN is the baby hero and an Irish boy to boot, so there is no wonder at the worship and admiration lavished upon him. Mr. Whitehead sings the early portion of the song with considerable spirit and in the last verse holds the rapt attention of the listener by his fine expressive manner. The individual style of this singer in his performance of this ballad is sure to attract considerable attention. (*Speed* 81.)

Published by Boosey & Co.

Old advertisement

Father playing the fool - Childhood memories of Brookfield

❏ Sunny summer Saturday afternoons spent at Brookfield Lawn Tennis Club, Rathgar, everybody playing dressed in white.

Children were not allowed to play tennis on Saturday afternoon, but nonetheless we enjoyed the occasion and of course the afternoon tea. Anyway I thought it was great, even if it was the age of children being seen and not heard. Really life then was much easier for both parents and children as we accepted the limitations and I for one never minded or felt deprived.

❏ Going with my father and brother to the Grafton Picture House to see one of the early talking pictures. It was so noisy, when we came out my father's comment was – "that will never take on!" Actually he loved the pictures, especially the Wild West ones and I spent many a happy hour with him in the Stella Picture House in Rathmines.

❏ I associate most of our fun outings with my father, but once I became a mother I realised that my mother was always there for us, preparing lovely meals and indeed responsible for the smooth running of the home. Both of them supported me in all my activities. Though they were very different in disposition I never heard any rows, only my father's impatience when he had to wait for her before attending some function or visiting socially. Time was never so important to her. As a teacher he lived by the clock as I did for years, even now I find it hard to cope with unpunctuality.

❏ A typical example of my parents' dispositions - one day I fell down a steep flight of stairs to the kitchen, carrying a loaded tray. Needless to say it was a noisy descent. My father rushed out from a room upstairs calling "Isolde, are you alright?" My mother appeared from the kitchen concerned as to what might be broken, apparently unconcerned about me!

❏ Christmas Eve – having lunch with my father in Roberts' Café in Suffolk Street. Only men were allowed in the downstairs section but obviously an exception must have been made for me. My favourite food there was iced buns and Eccles cakes. I have never tasted as good since. As a family we all then went to the Grafton Picture House and afterwards had tea, saw the lights in O'Connell Street and came home on the tram, tired but excited about Christmas Day.

❏ My brother and I had pillowcases at the end of our beds instead of stockings. About 3.00 a.m. on Christmas morning he would wake me, carry my full pillowcase to his bedroom where we opened our presents. We were usually found fast asleep in the morning surrounded by our gifts and wrapping paper. Christmas Day had to fit in with my father's arrangements, as he was singing morning and afternoon in Christ Church Cathedral. Thus our Christmas Dinner was in the evening, which as children was more unusual and special for us. We always had a jigsaw to do in the evening and we enjoyed this so much and found it very relaxing. I to this day still love puzzles. Both of my parents were keen stamp collectors and that is still a major hobby of mine.

❏ As teenagers a few of us used to cycle up to the Dublin mountains on Saturday afternoons, a really gruelling effort but well worth it for the fact that we could free-wheel back virtually the whole way down to Rathfarnham. We also cycled to Ballymoney for some of our camping trips. In fact we cycled everywhere. Tramlines were on many roads, in city and suburbs and were the cause of many of our falls; of course there were much fewer cars than nowadays, otherwise we wouldn't have lasted long!

1935 – 1938

Being born of British parents, it was natural that my mother should take me to London for the Silver Jubilee of King George V and Queen Mary in 1935. It was a wonderful spectacle and even more so from our point of view, as there was no such thing as television and the papers only had black and white pictures. I loved London, my mother's brother, Alfie, lived there and he organized both cultural and fun trips, including the theatre; one of the shows being Ivor Novello's 'King's Rhapsody' in which Novello played the lead. Each day Uncle Alfie gave us instructions, be it for the bus or tube as to how to get to the various things that he had organized. We were both really spoilt. I kept a note of our expenses and looking back I see that we could have a good lunch for a shilling or a little under.

On the day of the Jubilee we had seats in an upstairs room over a shop in Oxford Street, so we had a really perfect view of the whole procession, but my mother wasn't satisfied with this so we decided that we would go to the Embankment to see the return trip. We found a place; mind you it wasn't the best, where we could watch the procession on the return journey. What with the heat and the crowds, my mother passed out and had to be taken to the St. John's Ambulance Emergency post. There she recovered after a while and saw the entire procession from an upstairs window, she got a lot of teasing about that, we thought her timing was excellent!

Two years later my mother and I repeated the trip for the Coronation of King George VI and Queen Elizabeth. Once again a great occasion. This trip was shortly before I sat my Senior Cambridge and I was only allowed miss school with a threat hanging over me that I had better not fail my exams, as I would be in real trouble. Fortunately I made it.

Having completed my schooling, I still hankered after a life of physical activity. My mother thought I should take a nice safe job in the bank, but the thought horrified me. I was offered a part-time job as games mistress assistant in Alexandra College, which I accepted with delight; at least it was an excuse for not settling down. I mainly coached hockey and obtained my Leinster Umpire's Certificate, I personally played lacrosse, cricket and netball. We were lucky enough in college to have as our games mistress, a former English test cricket player; needless to say we were all inspired to play cricket and to this day, I still love it.

I played in the first ladies cricket match of selected teams in Ireland. I managed to get a full toss ball on the eye and had to be taken to Baggot Street Hospital to have my eyelid stitched. This was done by a Dr. Jamie Clinch, who was at that time a well-known rugby player, but also very well known for the fact that it took him about fourteen years to become a doctor, so everybody was a bit worried as to how I'd look after the job he did on me. To be fair, there was absolutely no trace of a scar after he had stitched it. The report in the Irish Times the next day was quite amusing, it quoted that Miss Whitehead had a very good idea of overarm bowling, but lacked sense of direction, however I did get credit for dismissing three of the opposition. This caused much amusement, but I'm afraid it was true. I think at that stage most of us were still bowling underarm, I was trying to do it the proper way – overarm, so the ball was not always going where I aimed it!

Alexandra College Cricket Team
Sheila standing 1st left, I am sitting 2nd left

WOMEN'S CRICKET

FIRST OFFICIAL MATCH

◆

MISS FOX HITS OUT AT SYDNEY PARADE

◆

The first official women's cricket match held in Dublin resulted in a win for Miss Ennis's XI. over Miss Howard's XI. by 50 runs at the Pembroke ground last evening. The idea of getting our athletic girls interested in cricket is commendable, and once they have overcome a feeling of strangeness—for, after all, cricket is unlike any other game—they will play it with more skill and more enjoyment. Most of them can already hit the ball well and truly on the leg side, but off strokes proved rather too difficult.

The bowling, naturally enough, was the weakest feature. Miss Whitehead has an excellent idea of over-arm bowling, but at present she lacks a sense of direction. Miss Ennis and her fellow-bowlers resorted to more feminine but on the whole more effective under-arm deliveries, which were generally pitched on the stumps, and the fielding of her side was distinctly better; in fact, it was very good indeed. In this respect Miss Jesse was outstanding for Miss Howard's side.

Miss Fox, sister of the Phœnix players, hit out boldly for her 47 runs, and Miss Parsons and Miss Pemberton, sister of W. C. Pemberton, also batted well, but the most knowledgeable bat on either side was Miss Whitehead, who never looked like getting out until she was unlucky in being struck by a full-pitch ball on the face. There are, I hear, to be other matches, and the standard of play should show a big improvement with every game. Scores:—

MISS ENNIS'S XI.

Q. Bain b Whitehead	11	D. Ennis not out	3
U. Fox b Whitehead	47	E. O'Kelly not out	6
C. Parsons b Howard	25		
D Pemberton c and b Whitehead	17	Total (4 wkts.)...*109	

* Innings declared.

Did not bat—S. Sheppard, B. Magee, N. Kelly, R. Hennessy, I. O'Kelly.

Bowling—Whitehead 3 for 24, O'Kelly 0 for 24, Howard 1 for 41, O'Reardon 0 for 15.

MISS HOWARD'S XI.

Whitehead retired hurt	17	Hanna b Magee	6
Gallagher b Ennis	0	Daly c I. O'Kelly b Ennis	3
O'Kelly retired hurt	2	Hickey b Ennis	0
Jesse b Magee	2	Skelton not out	19
Howard b Ennis	2	Extra	1
Maguire c E. O'Kelly b Ennis	6	Total	59
O'Reardon c E. O'Kelly b I. O'Kelly	1		

Bowling—Ennis 5 for 12, Magee 2 for 3, I. Kelly 1 for 12.

Newspaper Cutting - The Irish Times 1937

My brother Dallas was appointed as a Quantity Surveyor to the British Air Ministry in Singapore on a two-year contract. When war broke out he tried to get into the Air Force but was turned down because of his eyesight. Instead he stayed in Singapore and was lucky to get out with all his belongings just before the Japanese invaded Malaya, in all he was there 4 years. He shipped home some lovely carved furniture and beautiful vases most of which I now have. He worked in various air ministries in England and Northern Ireland. He died in England in 1982, aged 67, after a long fight with throat cancer.

My brother Dallas

The Women's League Of Health And Beauty

Mrs. Bagot Stack, the daughter of one of the founders of the Dublin Dental Hospital, had witnessed and experienced during the First World War the emergence of women from the protection of the home to wider fields of opportunities and responsibility. She realised that the new opportunities were destined to alter the pattern of women's lives everywhere and that attempts must be made to aid women in the process of adaptation to new conditions and new circumstances. She believed, moreover, that in addition to the increasing facilities for general education that were already coming into being, special attention would have to be given to health education. Sport and physical training were recognised as an

Mary Baggot Stack
Founder of The Women's League of Health and Beauty

Prunella Stack O.B.E.
Daughter of the founder and President of the organization

essential part in the education of young men, but corresponding facilities for young women were woefully inadequate. Much of what was being done in the schoolroom was adapted from systems created primarily for men and in many cases taught by ex-servicemen.

From small beginnings in 1930 the Women's League of Health and Beauty today is an international movement with centres in England, Scotland, Ireland and Wales as well as New Zealand, South Africa, Pakistan and the Netherlands. It is now known as the Fitness League, except in Ireland, where it remains The League of Health. Its genius lies in the simplicity of exercises to music, which brings within the reach of all, experience of movement to music hitherto reserved for the student of dance. The League is essentially an organisation for the advancement of physical education for women and children and is based on the system of remedial and recreative exercises initiated by Mrs. Bagot Stack. The programme of exercises, which was developed, stressed the importance of carrying the principles learned in classes into everyday activities. It was intended that the League should be a vehicle through which the system could reach women throughout Britain and, eventually, the world.

The League is not just a 'youth movement'. The exercises are designed to serve women throughout their lives. The typical League centre includes in its membership women of all ages, and the classes are among the relatively few recreative activities that can be continued through-out life. All the League exercises are eminently suitable for men too. Children from the age of two years are taught through the medium of play exercises. They will learn correct posture, which will stand to them all their lives.

The League exists through the support of its members and the enthusiasm of its teachers, who work in close co-operation with the medical profession. Many members are sent to the classes by their doctors for the physical and mental benefits which accrue. All League teachers have to do a minimum of two years part-time training before becoming fully qualified and have to have a thorough understanding of how the body works.

Today's emphasis on slimming, back to nature and relaxation in a world where speed and pressures crowd in on the individual from all sides has highlighted the League's way of life and this unique organisation continues to prosper after seventy years. So many people take on physical activities far beyond their individual capabilities often ending up with injury or being thoroughly disheartened at their inadequacies. The exercise that hurts is rarely a good one. To exercise aerobically one must be physically fit first. The League's sense of tradition, the high calibre of its teachers and its worldwide membership puts it in a class of its own.

MOVEMENT IS LIFE — a photograph of Peggy St. Lo
chosen as the emblem of the League

"Movement is Life" - our worldwide motto

Kathleen O'Rourke

Kathleen O'Rourke was amongst the first in Ireland to stress the importance of physical exercises for adults and children of all ages. She had graduated from the Liverpool College of Physical Education with a first class diploma and later trained at the Bagot Stack Health School. For a time she had been a member of the Central Council of Sports and Physical Recreation in Scotland, and had represented Ireland at the International Conference of Education in London. Kathleen also qualified as a Remedial Gymnast at Pinderfields General Hospital, Yorkshire, and worked as a physiotherapist.

In 1934 Kathleen brought the Women's League of Health and Beauty to Ireland. The name was changed later to The League of Health Ireland. Mrs. Stack was too ill to travel for the inauguration, so her daughter Prunella, aged 20, took her place. Kathleen had many obstacles to overcome. Firstly, our logo of Peggy St. Lo, leaping on the beach was frowned on by the Roman Catholic Church, her clothing was pretty flimsy, so we weren't allowed to use it. Special badges had to be made with "Dublin Centre" stamped on them in place of the "leap", later it was changed to "Ireland" as the

Demonstration Team 1936 (Kathleen front left)

League grew. Our uniform was not considered adequate, so we wore short skirts, which actually looked much worse when we were upside down!

I had not joined the League at this stage but Kathleen often talked about her uphill struggle, which was made even more difficult by the fact that she was related to Archbishop McQuaid. Finally the word "Beauty" was thought to give the wrong impression. I am not sure when the word "Beauty" was dropped, but my father used to tell everybody it was the year I qualified. He could never resist the quick retort. Our logo "Movement is Life" is very important to us.

In 1947 Kathleen O'Rourke founded the Dublin College of Physical Education (DCPE), which was recognised by the Department of Education. At that time the fees were £80 per year. It was a three-year training, involving sports as well as the Bagot Stack system of exercises and the ethos of that organisation. In 1955 it was amalgamated with St. Raphael's College of Physical Education and moved to Sion Hill, Blackrock. She found the new environment restrictive and resigned in 1958. Some years later the college was transferred to Limerick, where it eventually became Thomond College. Here, sadly, there is less and less emphasis on physical education and more and more on academic subjects. Though this may seem a good idea, it has resulted in less physical activity for children. Physical exercises and posture training, as distinct from sports and games are not compulsory as a secondary school subject. No wonder posture is deteriorating and obesity increasing.

Kathleen was training the students and I was assisting her, especially with music, which has always been an essential part of our work. I also coached swimming and some of those students became excellent swimming teachers.

After their three-year training, which was completed in 1950, some of the students were employed as physical education teachers in schools. As a result the League was taught to the children and many of them are now adult members of the League. A further three-year course was completed before Kathleen moved to Sion Hill.

Kathleen was becoming more and more involved with training mothers for natural childbirth. Much of our basic work could be so easily adapted for both pre- and post-natal work. There are many women who have reason to be grateful to her for the help she gave them. At that time she was not accepted by the majority of the medical profession and indeed resented by many nursing staff. Being Kathleen she did not allow this to interfere with what she considered of vital importance and personally attended many of her clients during labour. She had a small upstairs flat in Upper Pembroke Street and it was here and in the Coombe Hospital that she held these classes. Now, as we know, it is recommended for all pregnant women to attend ante-natal classes. These are usually carried out by a physiotherapist.

In the early 1950s we had a polio epidemic, many people young and old died or were very badly disabled as a result. Kathleen very soon realised that for some people, if they were treated quickly enough, the paralysis might be reversed. Again her little flat became a mini clinic. A chance encounter with Lady Valerie Goulding began a relationship, which was to culminate in the founding of the Central Remedial Clinic – Kathleen as the hands on operator and Lady Goulding as the fundraiser and promoter. In 1954 the Clinic moved to Goatstown and finally to Vernon Avenue, Clontarf in 1968, where it is today. This building was officially opened by President de Valera.

To quote Lady Goulding at the time of Kathleen's death "I feel very much that over the years Kathleen's work has not been fully appreciated, her life was given up to helping others. If there had not been a Kathleen O'Rourke there would never have been a Central Remedial Clinic".

Now they have both died but their legacy is enormous.

Of course all this meant that Kathleen had less and less time to teach League classes as more and more of her time was taken up working at the clinic and also her ante-natal classes. Because of this I had to take considerable responsibility for running the League. Lavinia McCarthy was teaching in Donnybrook, Maura Nyhan in Bray and Dorothie Malone in Mount Merrion, all three had trained in the D.C.P.E. I would have found it very hard to cope without Dorothie who had trained under Kathleen in the first course. She remained devoted to the League; she never really wanted responsibility but was always willing to do anything to help – her loyalty to me and her support continued until her sudden death in 1999. Lavinia and Maura no longer teach in the League, but Lavinia is still a well-known swimming teacher.

Until the arrival of taped music, we had the wonderful services of really talented pianists, including Madge Bradbury, Jane Hess, Julia Grey, Mary Braid, Sheila Murray, Ita Flynn and May Dalton. Their expertise and interest in the classes made a huge contribution to our success for which I will always be grateful.

My Training

In 1937 my mother had joined the Women's League of Health and Beauty. There is no doubt that Mrs. Bagot-Stack was years ahead of her time. Certainly in Ireland we were pioneers of her work, those of us who were involved and benefited from her basic exercises have carried it right through our lives. Is it any wonder that the League has survived all these years, while numerous other organisations and methods have come and gone.

When my mother joined, she tried to persuade me to join with her; being a typical teenager, I couldn't imagine enjoying something that my mother liked. How wrong I was. From the very first class I loved it and was immediately encouraged by Kathleen O'Rourke to do as many classes as possible. She was determined that I should train as a teacher. Once Kathleen decided on something, nothing could stop her and from then on my life revolved around the League; even I didn't realize that this was the start of my life-long dedication to the League and its ethos. At that time the classes were held in the Swiss Chalet in Merrion Road, Dublin. By modern standards the conditions were not great. We always work in bare feet, so after a few minutes the soles of our feet were black. Sitting or lying was somewhat hazardous, the floor was very splintery, not only did we get splinters in the seat of our pants, but our calves were riddled with them, in fact I used to spend ages picking them out of my legs and I marvel that I never had any ill-effects.

My parents needed a lot of persuasion to allow me to go to London to train, but eventually they agreed. Because of Kathleen's recommendation I didn't have to have an interview. In September 1938 I set out for London, travelling by boat and train. Relations of a friend of mine were putting me up in their flat for a few days until I found accommodation. I was excited but nervous. The first morning I had to report to the League Headquarters in Mortimer Street. I arrived to find a notice saying that the college was closed due to the threat of war, but was opening a week later. This was at the time when Neville Chamberlain went to Berlin to talk to Hitler, where he negotiated a deal that Hitler would not proceed with annexing any more countries. How wrong we were to believe in any of this! A letter had been sent to me from the college, but I left Dublin before it had arrived.

Well, there I was, stranded with nowhere to go. Fortunately my bachelor Uncle Alfie, who lived in a men's club, helped me to find accommodation in a YWCA. It was not exactly home from home. I had a cubicle in a large bedroom, got breakfast and an evening meal and was allowed one bath a week. On my very limited budget, it was the best I could do. Eventually I was introduced to the Green Cross Club, which provided accommodation for students and girls on a low income. Here I shared a room with two others and was much happier. One of my room-mates, Eileen, remained a life-long friend until her death a few years ago.

My parents each wrote to me once a week. These are excerpts from some of the letters I received from my father during my first term.

❏ Reference to 'U A' or 'Unc A' in my father's letters, of course, refer to my Uncle Alfie. Over the years they used to make rude remarks about each other, which explains some of the comments.

September 1938

Vers Libie

We are glad that our petlet arrived safely in London
For if she had not, her future would have been very much undone,
Had she not got into Euston alright
Dad, Mammy and Mary* would have got a noticeable fright.

We are glad that our lambkin now learns from Prunella,
Who, from all that we hear seems a helluva fella –
(I am writing all this while I wait for my dinner,
Which is pretty tough luck on the blooming breadwinner)

* Mary was our family help for many years

We are glad that our petkin (or lambkin) is happy
And we hope that she's using the towel and nappy **
(pronounced serviette – not what you thought!)
That mammy provided the day that she left
To travel to England leaving the rest of the family jolly well bereft.

We are glad that this poem is now nearly finished
May our lambling in London have joys undiminished.
Get to bed soon at night, rise betimes in the morning
Keep an eye on Uncle Alf – That's our one word of warning.

23/10/38

My dear Isolde,

This is my birthday – only the wrong month! I've just had a chat with O'Donovan on the phone & he told me of your miraculous meeting at Windsor surely the world is a small place (Striking Phrase No 1.) As a matter of fact I was telling him the tale about how sorry you were you couldn't speak to him more coherently from "Pamela's" phone when he took the feet from under me (S.P. No 2) by relating his story. Truth is stranger than fiction (S.P. No 3).

The most striking phrase I know is "Strike whilst the iron is hot" & the most arresting "Stand and deliver"!!! Joking aside I could, I think, suggest a phrase if I knew what the public speech was to be about but its no use saying "Hell has no fury like a woman scorned" (Congrese) when you really meant "She looks as if butter wouldn't melt in her mouth" (Swift). If there's any reading room or library in the vicinity get a copy of "Familiar quotations" compiled by Barlett & you'll get more concentrated wisdom in 10 minutes than you realised existed.

A very appropriate saying for the present is Benjamin Franklin's ... "in this world nothing is certain but death and taxes". That's really arresting, and some how death, at times, is kinder than the taxes (that's an original one – O yet it is striking enough for a speech on over-taxation.) If I got wound up, ducky, I could write any amount of wisecracks, so could you if you put your dear little scatterbrain to its proper uses. Indeed, the sayings just come. One does not sit with a towel round one's head waiting for them. And if you want the most beautiful phrases of all, read your Bible. "So teach us to number our days that we may apply our hearts unto wisdom".

This isn't a lecture, dear, but when you start me off on such a subject I hardly know where to stop. You know I'm not churchily religious, but I do love beautiful things, & people who live clean and proper lives. Jesus said, "Love your neighbour as your self" & also told us to do nothing that would cause our brother to stumble. To cultivate a love of beauty, never do a mean thing, be courteous to your elders & considerate to those whose path in life is not so smooth as yours. And all the nice things we have heard of you since you left will be more than fulfilled. Privately – very privately you know – Mammy & I are rather proud of you & Dallas, & in these ultra modern days such a pride is excusable, I think. We hear of so many cases of unfortunate parents & ungrateful children.

Will you tell Unc A. that the contour of his face annoys me & that I don't think much of his superficial area.

30/10/38

My dear Isolde,

I'm hurt: With reference to my dealing with your last letter you told Mammy to forget it. You asked for striking phrases and you got them. You're a thankless little 'ussy and only for the fact that I've nothing whatever to tell you I wouldn't be writing now.

I'm in the breakfast room (a weird place at 7 pm of a Sunday) but Truda is above & I know I couldn't consecrate my mind if I had to listen to a fire of cross talk, so I retired gracefully downstairs in order to coagulate with my daughter.

Uncle Alfie

*As a matter of fact there is singularly little news: Mammy &
I went to see "A Yank at Oxford" & got a good laugh out of
it & on Friday the O'Donovans came in for Bridge. He
plays but indifferent well, & managed to lose 3/7. He also
very nearly pulled poor old Father down too, but I
managed, on change of partners, to improve a little &
finished only 5d down on the night. The 5d, of course,
went to Mammy.*

*I do hope the swimming coaching is not so expensive as to
become a luxury – It's the one thing I'd like you to be able
to take advantage of. (Hope you like the sentence).
Heaven knows you haven't many gifts, talents, attributes or
mental physical endowments, but propelling yourself
through the water at a slightly quicker pace than the
average seems to be one of your peculiarities – plus the
ability to fall off a 3 metre board headfirst – so you might
as well foster, cherish, promote, advance, stimulate and
forward such innate capabilities as you possess (Whew!)*

At this point tell Uncle A. that I still can't bring myself to regard him as anything but pure dud.

From your letter your days seem to be rather full up but we have recognised this in letting you off with one letter a week. The funny part about it is that Dallas' letter came 1st post on Saty – your at 10 a/m same day & at 11 ock I wandered in disconsolately from the garden & said to Mammy "It seems a long time since we heard from the youngsters, doesn't it?" said in joke no doubt, but with an underlying truth. We love the pair of you so much that we are just re-living our lives in you. Our thoughts are simply always with you & Dallas, & we just wait from one letter to another, content in the knowledge that you are both happy & doing congenial work. It's a source of great satisfaction to us and tempers the loneliness, which we cannot help but feel.

Saw Raymond on Friday & gave him a lift. His Father must be annoyed about you for I've had no word of the promised plants. Raymond was wearing a brown pork pie chapeau and looked trés chic. - & incidentally he asked after you & I told him you were in London. "No" ses he, elevating his eyebrows until I thought his hat would become detached. "Mais oui" said I in Irish : so he subsided.

Having dealt with your last letter, in which there was little of note and less to answer (that's one I've got back on you!) I must get up to Truda & play for her while she dislocates her patella.

I know I'm foolish – but I do love you:

As ever

Daddy

27 Nov '38

My dear Isolde

Well, dear, three weeks today you'll be sitting here giving out the pay. I've tried my best to keep my end up (I don't mean what you mean) with mammy but I don't think I'll be able to survive another female. I'll simply be submerged.

We couldn't quite understand your reference to the coach's answer to your remarks re fees. Do you mean that she'll send in her bill when you are able to swim??? I note you had two dives off a lovely board – not two lovely dives off a board. There's a big difference.

Someone was asking after you the other day & I told them that I admired you. Daddies naturally love their daughters but when admiration of a daughter's conduct can be added, the result reaches a rather fine total. All we are longing for is for you to be at home, getting it all off your chest - & you certainly should have a lot to tell us, apart from your weekly epistle.

I presume you don't expect to be thrown out at the end of this term. They'll likely keep you on until Easter before they realise how bad you really are!

Did you see the account in the press of an auction of wine & spirits in aid of some charity? All the bigwigs ransacked their cellars & sent bottles of their choicest vintages. Gracie Fields said she was inclined to favour temperance & sent a bottle of minerals! I thought that was just lovely.

I hope to write UncA any time now. I've had rather a lot to do this past week & hadn't time to send him the usual carefully polished literary production which it is generally his privilege to receive from me. Sorry & all that.

Be good – or, rather, go on being good.

> *Love from*
>> *Daddy*

4/12/38

There's singularly little news this end. Mammy's having some strenuous golf, bridge and whist, but she's keeping in good training & she's reduced her thinking time for declaring trumps by several minutes.

We sent on another dance invitation & Miss Joynt was asking when you'd be home as she wants to send you an invitation for Student's Night. By the way wouldn't it be just as well, or even better, if you made out a list of the days and hours on which we might expect to see you? I'd love to play darts with you – what about booking 8 pm on the 32nd Dec. So far as I can see it's your only spare time.

As I said to Dallas, we expect a spate of news from you when you get home that even the Poulaphuca dam won't hold up.

Our first term was a trial term, so at the end we were all interviewed and told whether or not we could continue our training. Only twelve of us were accepted. During Christmas holidays Kathleen asked me to teach the Monday classes for her. I can't remember the excuse she gave for not teaching but I believed her at the time. Looking back I think she was testing me out. I taught all Monday afternoon, had a three quarter hour tea break and taught until 10.00 p.m. In the first half hour I had taught everything I knew. My pianist was Madge Bradbury who had known me from babyhood, as she was a pupil of my father's and sometimes accompanied him. She gave me great moral support and these sessions included tap dancing, which was no bother to me. Between us I got through, but it made me realize what was ahead.

I loved every moment of my time in London. Having a strong dancing background helped me enormously in the training. In the evenings we could demonstrate for teachers at their classes. This I loved doing and it gave me great experience. The League in England found it very hard to cope financially. Mrs. Stack had always wanted the classes to be within the reach of everybody, thus making it very difficult to expand with ever increasing costs.

During our first term Prunella Stack, daughter of our founder, had married Lord David Douglas Hamilton. In my second term I decided to run a dance and cabaret to raise money. Both attended

Training in London 1938/39

Teaching Staff at my training (London)
Left to right: Eileen McMurray, Marjorie Duncomb (now 100 years
old), Prunella, Joan and Peggy St. Lo

the occasion, she was really lovely and he, tall and very handsome, so you can understand that we were, as teenagers, completely bowled over. I had lost my voice, no doubt due to stress. Prunella must have asked David to dance with me, as the organiser. I have never forgotten the embarrassment of not being able to get out even a whisper while he gallantly tried to make conversation. Needless to say I was the envy of all my fellow students, they little realised how miserable I was. Otherwise it was a great success, I know we raised the magnificent sum of £23, at least it was magnificent then! Looking back I realise that the League was beginning to take over my life.

I was born with very short Achilles tendons. Eveline Burchill used to shout at me to lower my heels but I just couldn't. Also it came against me in springboard diving, as I had difficulty getting height from the board. It wasn't until I was training in London that the problem was recognised. Classical Greek Dance and the Medau running (exaggerated jogging movement) caused me a lot of pain. The specialist told me I would have to give up my training, otherwise they would eventually break and I would be crippled for life. I cried for days but was determined not to give up. I received the following from my father at the time:

Little Liz had a very short tendon,
Which she said she could ne'er get a bend on,
To the Clinic she fetched it
And then they soon stretched it
From Portland Street right out to Hendon.

And now she can dance like a sprite –
All she got was a horrible fright,
For even Miss Duncombe
Remarked 'twas all buncombe'
So everyone's merry and bright.

The following are more excerpts from my father's letters.

15/1/39

My dear Piglet/Petlet

> *Margaret is above stairs so I have retired to the breakfast room, with a supply of liquorice all sorts, to commune with my daughter.*

> *Since you went, the house has been as of the dead. I grant you, that things are somewhat tidier & that we are not continually tripping over photos of the Royal Family, yet sadness lurks in nooks and crannies & despair peeps from behind the doors. I stalk about like a gaunt spectre and Mammy's face registers continual weariness like Miss Duncombe. . . .*

> *I'm glad you received my note + poem in time to acknowledge them, but I was hurt when you said it (the poem) was a marvellous effort. It's no effort my dear. As I once said to Shelley, (his name was Percy too), right rhymes & rare rhythms run rippling from my pen and alliteration is my middle name. He was terribly impressed*

& sat down & wrote that epic poem. "A thing of beauty is a joy for ever". An example of direct inspiration. Keats helped him.

> *If your waist is far from neat*
> *And you suffer from flat feet*
> *And your form's the source of many a scornful shaft,*
> *Join the League of Health & Beauty*
> *"Do it now" * – it is your duty –*
> *(*Extract from a pubic notice!)*
> *And you'll soon be prepossessing – fore and aft.*

Of course I can't be continually pouring out these pearls of poetry – unless I receive adequate remuneration … I'm just tellin' yer.

If you go to the Welsh match on Saturday get near to the microphone and yell "Hello, Daddy". And Mammy & I will hear our little orphan!

22/1/39

My dear little Gosling –

Many thanks for your special letter, and hearty congratulations on your remarkable success. We are greatly intrigued as to what being head of the "Cs" means. Mammy thought you might have left a letter out before the "C" – meaning Wesleyan Chapel, or alternatively William Conqueror – but I didn't think so. Please lighten our darkness. But we do gather that you have been singled out from among your fellows - & if you aren't careful we'll begin to feel proud of you.

Mammy was very jealous when Mary handed me your letter, saying it was addressed to me. When the Mr. & Mrs. stunt is worked, Mammy, being the "lady" (at this point, cross yourself) bags the whole doings & I read the epistle on sufferance. On Saturday I told her exactly where she got off, on which she became rather contumacious and censorious. As I abhor truculence and bellicosity (that sounds nearly a rude word) I replied rather tersely, on which she evinced a spirit of vulgacity that was altogether reprehensible : And that was how the row started.

Which reminds me that this morning while shaving I observed a small white-topped excrescence on the point of my nasal promontory. I squeezed it in the approved manner & I've been getting along well ever since. I had a bit of a set back this afternoon but I'm feeling nearly alright now. These things are weakening, aren't they?

We listened in to the match yesterday & enjoyed it very much. Apparently the commentator is shut in his box for we heard no shrill girlish treble saying "Hello Daddy". You might like to add the following to your collection.

To see England well walloped by Wales yesterday
Alf and Olly proceeded to Twickenham.
But when England had finished with Woolles & Co.
The Welshman had divil a kick in 'am.

Our forwards were Marshalled by Taven & Toft
And their footwork – By gosh! Who could match it?
And when feelings felt flurried and fellows fell foul
There was Prescott to Barry the hatchet.

Witness Wheatley & Watkins a-wandering a round
With that great Husky – son of a gun –
There was fire in that eight that kept Wales in a state
And that cooked them until they were done.

Sorry I've no time to go thro' the whole team, but let that suffice.

I have turned over the question of tunics &c to Mammy. I'm glad to learn however that you've to get tights. What would be tights for you would be slacks for others! The one thing I'm in complete agreement is the 2nd shoes. You may have another pair.

Glad the broadcast sounded alright. As a matter of fact there was nearly a collapse thro' no fault of ours & I'm going to see the B'casting director tomorrow afternoon. I gave them the chord – very quietly – for one of the part songs & just as I'd finished the preliminary beats before coming in, a band practising below played a loud chord in any old key & naturally we staggered & nearly collapsed. Imagine allowing a band to rehearse in a room that wasn't sound proof. Providentially the right note stuck in my head, I sang it for the sopranos and inside a few seconds you wouldn't know anything had happened. But the shock nearly finished us. Trust 2RN.

For the rest, be a good 'ickle girlie & don't be harsh with the "Cs". Perhaps you'll tell us all about them in your next letter – also your swimming experiences.

Fond love from us both

As ever

Daddy

19 Feb 39

This was on the wireless last night. The comedian said they were going to have a fancy dress ball and one of the conditions was that all the girls had to have their dresses pinned on. He was going as a magnet!

12 Mar 39

In reply to your letter which we hope to get before long, I hardly know what to say in answer to the questions which you will in all probability ask : still it is better to answer an unasked query than not to reply to a question that has been asked – if you follow me – and so, in anticipation of the interrogation formulating in your brain (if any) I have to inform you here & now or there and then that the answer is in the infirmary. And now you know where you are.

I enjoyed my student days immensely. We covered so many subjects as well as most forms of dance. We had, of course, to study Anatomy and Physiology, also public speaking and mime. Financially it was very difficult but I knew my parents gave me what they could. After I had paid for my board, breakfast and evening meal, I had five shillings and sixpence left for lunches, writing home twice a week, transport (I regularly walked a mile to save a penny) and my weekly visit to Marshall Street Baths as I was training for the Irish Swimming Championships. I think I would not have coped without my Uncle Alfie, who took me to Lyons Corner House, Tottenham Court Road and then to the cinema, twice a week and now and again we had an outing on Sunday. My roommates and I used to save to put a shilling in the gas meter; the highlight of our weekends was to share half a pound of margarine and a crumpet each, which we toasted.

Looking back it was probably the best training I could have had and as the war years followed I learnt never to waste anything and always to enjoy the simplest of pleasures. Apart from my uncle making sure I was well fed, he brought me to all the main sporting venues. I saw cricket matches at Lords and the Oval, Rugby at Twickenham and the boat racing at Henley. I really loved it all, now I enjoy watching all these events on television so much more having been to the venues.

The year raced ahead with a break for Whit, Uncle Alfie took me to Bristol to his brother, my Uncle Ernie and his family. The sun shone the whole weekend and I returned to the training virtually black and somewhat embarrassed. Of course it all eventually peeled and I marvel that I never got skin cancer because we had no ideas of the dangers and used to lie in the blazing sun with no protection whatsoever. I was one of the lucky ones as I was dark skinned anyway.

Age 19 as a student

These are a final selection from my father's letters.

30/4/39

My dear little Fairy!

It seems strange settling down of a Sunday to write to you. It's hard to know whether it's more inconvenient to have you here or be forced to correspond with you hebdomadally (that has you : & it's nothing to do with abominable or abdominally). However, to return to our muttons, I duly delivered the parcel to Truda & she beamed all over. I suppose she will write you & give you a list of her presents. Apparently they did her proud. She asked did she look very old, so I said no – merely a bit bedraggled & careworn & advised that she have her face lifted : otherwise she was quite normal.

Yesterday we went to Newcastle Co Wicklow to visit Canon Long. They have 4 acres of a garden so I managed to come away with a plant or two! The drive was lovely. Incidentally they invited our "young folk" if they cared to come along & were greatly astonished to learn that one was in Singapore and the other in London. My youthfulness & prepossessing appearance coupled with my urbanity & general charm of manner make it hard for comparative strangers to realise that my children are of an age. Of course Mammy doesn't see eye to eye with me about these points & merely refers to me as a mutt : But then, was a fellow ever appreciated by his nearest & dearest.

14/5/39

My dear little Elf!

Just finished tea & tho' I've to arrange a program for Radio Eireann I must write to me pettikins (bother her). There is definitely no news so far as I am concerned. I rose up in the morning, went to the Feis, ate as opportunity occurred, & came home each evening tireder than ever & finally after the Omara Cup on Friday, I retired to Dugort dead to the world & didn't leave the house till this morning to go to the Cathedral. I even missed the Dramatic Cup on Friday night. I told you on the P.C. that we had won the

Cup outright. The adjudicator gave us unqualified praise: He said it sounded so easy: they merely sang, &, says he, the conductor did nothing! He was praising me because I didn't wave my arms about & get all het up. The choir certainly sang beautifully & I just conducted by giving them a look when the various parts had to come in, with just an odd movement of my hands to get more or less tone. He said our gradations of tone were excellent & so varied.

> *Affectionately*
>> *Daddy*

29/5/39

My dear Isolde,

This is the shortest ever but I don't want to break the sequence.

Y'day, Sunday, I spent at home with the father & mother of all colds & I couldn't write. At the moment Mammy & I are just starting for Wicklow Gap to lie out in the sun. It's a glorious day.

I'll make up for this later. I really couldn't write y'day as I was so cheerful that my letter would have been filled with funerals, sudden deaths & unjustifiable homicides.

We got your letter posted Bristol.

On Wed at 6.5 we broadcast : Listen if you can for an item or two.

Love from us both. Hope you had a good time in Bristol.

> *Your affectionate*
>> *Dad*

Wedy. 14 June '39

(Supposed to be written by my mother but really written by my father.)

My dear Isolde,

I know you would be disappointed if you didn't get the usual letter on Thursday so I feel I should write, as is customary. Daddy's in the garden working away – bless him. I often tell him he shouldn't go at it so hard because after all he's not young and his arteries aren't so soft as they used to be. But he just gives that wistful smile of his & carries on, tho' I can see he's just jaded.

Yesterday I was playing golf at Rathfarnham. The mixed doubles were on & my partner & I did very well, only losing the first 4 holes. I stayed on to a singsong in the evening & quite forgot Daddy would be home for dinner. But he never minds : In fact I have to coax him to eat ... but he's so patient. In over 27 years I've never heard him complain. You'll never have another father like him.

This morning I went into town to get some material for camisoles & would you believe it I couldn't get anything at Brown & Nolan or Hodges Figgises. They'd nothing in stock except Japanese Tweed & Waterproof sheeting & I always regard both these as rather heavy for lingerie. My new costume is lovely. It's XX length with the flounce cut on the bias & the colour is a sort of crushed sweet pea. I was trying to get Daddy to invest in a new suit but with that sad look in his tired eyes he said "No darling : what I have will last out my time : He's only had his present suit for 7 years & only that it's thin about the bottom end of the trousers it's nearly as good as new : and it's not paid for yet in any case." I do wish I could get him to take a little more interest in his appearance. Only yesterday I just stopped him going out with odd shoes on & his collar not fastened on behind. He looked so pathetic, poor dear, that it took me all my time to keep from kissing him. But the Dr. says he mustn't be subjected to any form of shock because his heart isn't strong, even tho' it's in the right place.

Well darling, I must stop as I've a lot of letters to write & pictures to go to & bridge to play. Daddy is tidying up the garden still. I do wish he'd come in & rest. But he says if he rests he rusts : so what can I do? Don't bother to answer this – by return.

With love

from

Mammy

25/6/39

(My mother was in London with me at this time)

Dear little Floweret!

Having written to you & Mammy rather recently I don't seem to have much news – especially as I have been busying myself about the house. Mammy says Auntie Ria is due on the 30th. (I thought Unc.A. was coming) so I bestirred myself to put a coat of paint on the bath. I hope after the final coat is put on that the business will dry sufficiently by Friday to enable Auntie to have a steep without sticking, or coming to the surface with large patches of bath enamel clinging to her person. And it makes such a mess on the towel. Then Haisly & I have been doing a job on the car, painting & varnishing, sundry portions. If you see one side you say that a Peugeot, if you see the other side you say that's a Rolls Royce : if you see the back side (like you going through a hoop.) you are merely rude. Then Mary said the stove in the kitchen wasn't drawing, so I bought me special cement & caulked up all holes in the flue & elsewhere. And now a regular gale whistles thro' it. I was telling Mammy that Mary was absolutely the business. There's only one thing about her that gets me down – viz when she sings. Having, over a period of years, attuned my ear to pleasant sound, I can assure you that I suffer acutely when she breaks into melody. If any one person could wreck The Tudor Ladies Choir I should put poor Mary an easy first. The only thing she'd blend with is a circular saw, and even then the saw could give her points. But in all other respects I give her best. If you think of it, send her a card to say you're alive. She showed me Mammy's card with evident pride.

And now sweet one – Sunday or no Sunday – I'm going to do a bit of painting. I'm looking forward to meeting Mammy at the N'Wall on Tuesday & it won't be so very long before I go & meet my only daughter. Hope you are feeling in good form for your Exams. How nice that Peggy St Lo should ask you to demonstrate (I can spell it).

2 July 39
So please do not worry
Nor get in a flurry
'Cos Eileen McMurray
Just asks you to hurry
And so forth.

My dear Duckling.

I've retired from the drawing room, as a running fire of conversation between Mammy & Auntie Ria would be too much for my lack of concentration. I met Auntie yesterday morning & by now she is quite acclimatised & returning to her food. (that reads strangely if you leave out the word "to"). And a fortnight today my little ducklet will be home & telling us how well she did in her exams. Don't worry, old sport, I'll love you just the same, even if Miss McMurray is harsh! It's rather good of you to come home on Sunday as I'll only have to write to you once again, while Mammy will have to agonise twice.

I haven't written since Mammy returned, have I? Of course I have had to mind my P's and Q's & I have again burst in verse.

When Ma returned, I went to meet the boat
My heart was in my mouth; a lump came in my throat,
She merely looked & said, "You sure do get my goat",
when she returned.

Since Ma returned, I dare not stay out late
Where once I lolled I now must sit up straight
Were I let sing I'd howl the Hymn of Hate,
since Ma returned.

Since she returned, my name is merely mud
My every hope is blasted in the bud
I'm told that from the neck up I'm pure dud,
since she returned.

Now she's returned, there's nothing I can say
She came to scoff – 'tis I remain to pray
I bow the head while she gives out the pay,
Yes! She's returned.

Tis a sad life & I'm sure that I have the cordial sympathy of you & your roommates.

Now I must go & join in the general festivities!

Again I hope you get nice questions during the next fortnight.

With love from us all

Your affectionate

Dad

9th July '39

My dear Daughtlet,

Your usual Saturdays epistle did not arrive, owing no doubt to an utter collapse of the British Postal Service & I feel as tho' I had no text to preach on – or from, as the case may be: and you know yourself that I must have news, otherwise I cannot write. However, we are living in hope that tomorrow morning's post will bring us word from our wee pet – the big ham – that she is still alive, after what must have been a fairly hectic week. Next Sunday we shall have you here, please goodness, with your troubles over & smiles radiating from every square inch of your old pie-face.

Auntie Ria is having a good time (I think) & eating well (I'm sure). Believe me, Little Auntie with the little appetite is a myth. She takes all that's coming & then some. The weather has been bad but we managed one nice trip in the region of Hell Fire! And on Friday we went round Dalkey & Killiney & did the pictures at the Pavilion, Kings Laoghairtown.   On the return journey we pointed out where our darling swum and doved.

Did you hear that I went in for that film stars doubles competition. I send my photo in as Ronald Coleman & got second prize – but the judge thought it was Wallace Beery. I wonder how they made the mistake.

And I said before, (or did I) nothing has happened since Mammy wrote on Wednesday. We eagerly await your news and if you don't hear from me in the meantime, I shall be hovering around the B & I on Sunday morning next, round about 8.00 – 8.15. I suppose you'll have to bring Uncle Alfie but will do our best to bear up. I note that he hasn't to work, blarst him, and as he can't look ornamental, I gather that we are in for a poor spell.

Till Sunday then

Affectionately yours

Daddy

In no time we were taking our first year exams, that is the Associate Teacher's exam and I managed to do well in all subjects. I went home with no idea that I wouldn't see London for years.

When sending me the first of the poems below, my father explained:

"I can turn out poems at reasonable prices but I charge extra when I illustrate them as below. I think the accompanying verse very neatly describes the object of the League – to do away with tails – and I would suggest that the figure I have depicted should be labelled 'before' (not 'behind') and the figure on your badge might be designated as 'after'. This will show what the League is supposed to do. This will cost you 7/6d.

If your big about the srat
And your contour hides your feet
'Cos your Diaphragm is bulbously inclined –
Join the League of Health & Beauty,
Ere your figure gets too fruity,
Just to mortify the flesh stuck on behind.

Monday : As ever was.

Your letter came. Oh, sunlit morn!
And peace now reigns within –
'Tis you what has been sinned agen,
The Post what done the sin.

Ø second thoughts bring best!

Outbreak Of War

War broke out at the beginning of September 1939 and of course all training stopped. Kathleen was determined I should continue. As a special concession and because she was so highly thought of, I was allowed complete my training in Dublin. This involved my returning to Eveline Burchill to study ballet, tap and ballroom dancing, culminating in my passing my exams and becoming an Associate of the Imperial Society of Teachers of Dancing (A.I.S.T.D.). Also I did one year medical in Trinity, as well as Anatomy and Physiology with Kathleen and teaching practice where I got all the difficult classes to teach. I also opened my first centre in Dun Laoghaire, teaching children and their mothers in the Royal Marine Hotel.

Most of this travelling was done on my bike, sometimes necessitating three journeys to Dublin and back to Terenure in the day. It was not very surprising that I picked up an infection causing a deep-seated abscess in my thumb. I had to have it operated on and a draining tube inserted for seventeen days. Now it would be cured with a course of antibiotics but they had not been invented then.

Not long after that I developed Vincent's Angina, an infection of the gums, tonsils, etc. The only injection they could give me then was arsenic. I was really very ill for a month and was told that I would have to have my tonsils and teeth out when I was better. Over sixty years on and I still have the tonsils and most of my teeth! At this time my father was in a nursing home having his gall bladder removed, so my poor mother had a difficult time as she had been ordered not to tell my father how ill I was. I slowly recovered and was allowed my first outing to a dance on my twenty- first birthday, which was about a month later.

Ballymoney 1940 with Alec

Irish Diving Championships - Blackrock

By this time I had passed my final exams. I was in the throws of my first serious romance (Alec), we both loved dancing so every Saturday night we danced in the Gresham Hotel. I think the dinner dance cost twelve shillings and six pence and stopped punctually at midnight.

As it was now summertime, I spent many hours at Blackrock, training for the Irish swimming and diving championships, no matter what the weather; cycling each day from Terenure. Then I was one of the top lady swimmers and divers, the standard reached at that time would rank at the very bottom of the pile now. I suppose not really to be wondered at when compared with the facilities and training of the modern day athlete. I had won the Guide and University Swimming Championships and over the subsequent years I acquired 6 Irish Gold medals and one silver for swimming and diving.

The League In Ireland

In the early 1940s Kathleen taught in some of the convent schools, supervised by a nun, to make sure the girls didn't lift their legs higher than right angles to their body! This continued into the 1950s. Hard to believe now, isn't it? I taught in Rathmines Technical College where I was paid five shillings per hour, twice what I was getting in the League.

Slowly over the years, attitudes changed, we shed our skirts and recovered our logo and we are now very proud of the League Of Health Ireland, an organisation which has stood the test of time and benefited thousands of women and children, not only health wise but also the friendliness and support that is always there in abundance. Despite the war years we were lucky enough to be able to hold classes and expand our membership. This was largely achieved by having classes in some of the big firms and hospitals.

I look back and I wonder that I remained a dedicated teacher. A typical week found me teaching the nurses in the Meath Hospital, Dr. Steevens' Hospital, also Peamount Sanatorium on a Saturday night, when everybody else was enjoying themselves. I also had classes in Jacobs factory and Woolworths of Henry Street. One of my early centres was in Naas teaching in the Town Hall. It was incredibly cold there and I can still remember in winter sometimes wearing fur gloves while teaching! By then I had the use of my father's car. My mother did reception for me. We had tea in Naas and then I went to Peamount Sanatorium instead of on Saturday evenings. One night I had a puncture, the snow was falling and I couldn't change the wheel as the car kept sliding off the jack. I had a long trek until I found a house with a phone and called the A.A. My recollection is that we didn't get home until after midnight to be greeted by a very worried father. Needless to say Monday was not my favourite day!

I really wanted to make use of my dancing qualification so taught ballet, tap and acrobatics combined with League work to all ages of children every Friday afternoon.   Despite all this I was earning very little.   My father had a studio at the top of the old Pigotts building in Grafton Street.   One day there was a disastrous fire and his studio was destroyed.   I was looking for somewhere to give private lessons in Ballroom dancing.   We found a suitable room in Mills of Merrion Row and shared this for some time.

There was a demand amongst League members for Ballroom dancing lessons, all seemed sure that husbands and boyfriends would support it.   I agreed to take the class after League on a Thursday evening.   I knew there was quite a lot of support for this but was anxious all the same.   Attendance was very good, except that the balance of the sexes was not a success – twenty-seven women and Alec.   Fortunately he rose to the occasion and needless to say he was not short of a partner.   I can't remember how long I battled on but I have to admit we had a lot of fun.   I did have one other ballroom class in the old Presbyterian Association building in St. Stephen's Green, where I hired a hall, this was successful as I had a reasonable mix of both sexes.

In the early 1940s the League moved to Bewley's café in Grafton Street.   How Kathleen persuaded Bewleys to let us have the

1st Dublin League Demonstration 1936. (Kathleen - front left)

classes there I never really found out. Our evening classes on Mondays and Thursdays were held using the whole of the ground floor. This necessitated clearing all tables and chairs. We taught standing on the counter amidst the coffee urns. I can remember having one class with over a hundred in it. The room was L-shaped and I stood on the corner of the counter so that I could see and be seen by all. At least we had no splinters to contend with but our feet were black after one minute and we had to deal with the odd raisin but it was all worthwhile and great fun.

Nearly every year the League had a demonstration in the Mansion House, which was a good way of publicising the work. Having performed for years in Eveline Burchill's dancing shows, it was something I really loved. The next step up was a show in the boxing stadium; to this we invited a well-known Swedish gymnastic team. There followed numerous small demonstrations until we finally hired either the Gaiety Theatre or the Olympia. It was possible then to hire theatres for a matinee for a comparatively reasonable sum. We used our own pianist accompanied by the orchestra. Demonstrations continued, both big and small over the years.

On Wednesday and Friday afternoons we had classes upstairs in one of the small cafés, again teaching on the counter. I have a very vivid memory of the day I was teaching and we heard the

Age 21 - Mansion House

Olympia Theatre 1940s - I am in centre under banner

newspaper boys coming up Grafton Street shouting, "The war is over". Our emotions were so mixed, joy and yet sorrow at how many people had been lost, of course that was 1945 and the war with Japan was still going on.

Probably the best publicity of all was, and still continues to be, talks to various women's groups, involving them in some simple exercises and giving a very short demonstration of our work. Slowly but surely the League grew and necessitated the training of more teachers.

Gillian aged 2 (3rd from left) 1st League Class

The Lingiad

In 1949 during the first three-year training course, we were invited to represent Ireland at the International Health Festival, known as the Lingiad, in Stockholm. We were the only country not sponsored by its own government, so we had to hold many social events and raised over £1000 (a lot of money then). Despite the fact

*Major Killander, a famous Swedish sportsman, greets
the youngest camp follower of the Irish team to the Lingiad,
on arrival at Stockholm.*

or probably because of it we were very proud to be the first group of women to represent Ireland abroad in an International event.

Eventually twenty-four members and students travelled to Stockholm for twelve days in August 1949. Very few of us had flown before, the journey took thirteen hours with a change of plane in London and we flew at 13,000 feet, it seemed very high in 1949. Jack Cruise, at that time a well-known comedian and his wife flew with us, as she was one of our team. As I had my baby, Dallas, with me I stayed with the Irish 'Chargé d'Affair' and his wife – Mr. And Mrs. Warnock and they made it very easy for me. Gillian, then aged three and a half was looked after by my parents.

Unfortunately the weather was bad – cold and wet. For us the worst part was the parade through the streets and standing in the arena while the rain poured down. In many ways we were lucky – as we were a comparatively small group we performed in a couple of theatres so avoided much of the terrible conditions. Despite this we had a wonderful time. At that time of year there was only a few hours of darkness, so we had plenty of time to see Stockholm and its surroundings.

As Kathleen and I were leading the team we were invited to some wonderful functions, including a visit to the palace. We attended some big dinners, we sometimes dined around midnight and weren't home until 2 – 3 a.m. By then I was anxious to get home as I knew I had a hungry baby waiting for his night feed, fortunately he was a very good baby and though awake, just waited until I arrived.

Everybody was so good to me and I am afraid I got used to being looked after. The day we left, we were all at the airport waiting for the call to board, we all made our way to the plane when I heard a voice behind me asking "is this yours?" I turned round to see one of the airport officials carrying the carrycot containing my precious son – it took a long time for me to live that down! On the return I broke my journey in London, so that I could visit many of my relations whom I hadn't seen since before the war, and of course I wanted to introduce them to Dallas.

The Irish team preparing for Stockholm

Preparing for Stockholm - Truda

INTERNATIONAL LINGIAD IN SWEDEN

By Kees van Hoek

FIFTEEN thousand gymnasts from 17 nations are taking part in the world'e second Lingiad, which has assembled in Stockholm.

STOCKHOLM, Sunday.

The Lingiad takes place every ten years. The first, just before the war, commemorated the 100th anniversary of the death of Per Henrik Ling, known as the "Father of Gymnastics," and the event is named after him.

Representatives go, not to compete for prizes, but to demonstrate physical training, and to learn as much as possible from other teams taking part.

The smallest team are the 13 from Brazil; the largest (from outside Sweden) 3,000 from Denmark. Britain has a contingent of 750 and France sent 100. Apart from teams, 66 nations have sent to Sweden leaders in public health, sport and education to act as official delegates and observers.

Ireland, however, is represented only because of the initiative of a small band of sport lovers. A group of Dublin businessmen guaranteed an overdraft for the £500 which was still needed after those taking part had collected £1,000 by their own efforts.

Only one among all the arrivals had a front-page picture in almost every Swedish newspaper—the 11-week-old baby of Mrs. Isolde McCullough, who is in Ireland's League of Health team. Sweden's famous sportsman, Major Killander, was at the airport to welcome them with the reception committee for the Irish, waving tiny tricolours. A huge Irish tricolour is flying in the centre of Stockholm from the bridge leading to the Royal Palace. In the Stadium, the three youngest States hold the central place of honour among flags of all the nations, Ireland between India and Israel.

IRISH TEAM

The Irish team has given so far two special performances by itself one of them in the Royal Theatre. Entering to the air of "O'Donnell Abu," which fascinated the audience, they performed their rhythmic exercises, formed into a design of a Celtic Cross. Irish airs were played throughout; many of them were sung—one in Irish —" Mo Teaglac." Kathleen O'Rourke, the leader of Ireland's League of Health, was in charge, and Julia Gray, the Dublin Gaiety pianist, was also there.

The 24 Irishwomen vary in age from 19 to 40. Seven of them are married; three are mothers. The youngest member is Anne Lucas, of Monkstown, who is training as a League teacher. Ann Lillis, a daughter of the late banker, finds herself taken for a Swede, and Mrs. Jack Cruise, who is well tanned, proves that there is such a thing as summer in Ireland.

Many of the team have never been away from Ireland before, and they have not yet overcome their wonder at the richness and cleanliness of Stockholm. But all of them find the very clear northern light hard on the eyes.

The Irish-Swedish Society (over which the former Swedish Consul-General in Dublin, Nils Jaenson, presides) has gone out of its way to make the team feel at home there.

Newspaper Cutting - August 1949

With Dallas, while rehearsing for the Lingiad
on the top of the Irish Times building in Dublin.

Family

In July 1943 I married Ken McCullagh, whom I had first met when I was fifteen. He was Irish 100 metre breaststroke champion in 1928 and founded the Royal Lifesaving Society in Ireland (R.L.S.I.). He encouraged me to take the R.L.S.I. exams including the Instructors certificate. He also coached me for the swimming championships. Most galas were held in Iveagh Baths. I regularly gave exhibitions of different swimming strokes and various tricks. Sometimes I was joined by Sheila and we demonstrated together. Looking back I suppose it was the early days of synchronised swimming but hardly compares with the teams that perform now! Ken and I were both members of Pembroke Swimming Club and at one stage were men and ladies captains respectively. He was an official in the Northern Bank in Newry.

Shortly before our marriage he was transferred to Dublin where he remained for the rest of his career. I continued to teach and I am sure the Bank was aware of this despite it being frowned upon for a wife to work. I was very relieved to be left in Dublin.

In February 1946 our daughter Gillian was born in Hatch Street Nursing Home (what an appropriate name!) I was so thrilled to have a daughter, the culmination of my dreams.

I was a fortnight in the Nursing Home, most of the time in bed and looked after by my own nurse, who returned home with us for a further fortnight – what luxury. Nowadays a mother has, at most, three days in hospital and then home to cope as best she can, even if there are other children to look after.

Three years later my son Dallas was born. My father was music professor in Alexandra College at the time. We discovered that our respective windows faced each other, so every morning at 11.00 a.m. we would wave to each other. I was out of bed straight away and back rehearsing within three weeks for the International Health

Doon - our first home in Mounttown with Gillian in pram

Ken, Gillian, me and Bomber

Gillian's Christening

Ken and Gillian

Festival to be held in Stockholm. In three short years the whole approach to childbirth had radically changed. I was fortunate to have James Quin as my gynaecologist. He was a great admirer of the League work. But for his encouragement I doubt if I would have considered travelling to Sweden, as I was breast-feeding Dallas. It hadn't occurred to me that I could take such a young baby with me.

I was delighted to have the family I had always wanted. Dallas was an exceptionally placid baby, my father used to talk to him in his pram and Dallas would smile at him and kick with pleasure. I often thought it strange that my father would turn to me and say, "I am so looking forward to when he is six months old." He died only a few days before Dallas reached that landmark.

My father (2 months before his death) and mother - August 1949

In many ways my father was very down to earth and never wanted a fuss. Even in his famous singing days he made little of it. As John McCormack said of him "he is the finest baritone that Ireland has ever had and he could be world famous". Harry Plunkett Greene – a well-known English singer and adjudicator considered he was the greatest interpreter of folk songs in the British Isles. All my father wanted was to make a reasonable living for his wife and children. His wish was to 'die in harness'.

Because of my father's profession we met many well-known people such as artists and writers and indeed I own some of their pictures. Like many artists, writers, musicians, etc. they only become famous after their death, which seems so sad to me. Two of my wedding presents, which I especially treasure, are paintings by Kitty Wilmer O'Brien and Howard Knee.

I also knew Norah McGuinness as a struggling artist, now her paintings, of which I have two, are sought after. Patrick Pye, I knew as a small boy and as I was ten years older I was detailed off to entertain him when his mother visited us; I am quite sure he doesn't remember this and it is only recently I discovered that he is an artist of some repute. The writer Maurice Walsh was a regular visitor; his books were very popular at the time.

Maurice Walsh

Wedding Presents

Irish Landscape - Kitty Wilmer O'Brien

Howth Harbour - Howard Knee

My father - last studio photo 6/5/37

One Sunday in October 1949 my father and mother were having lunch with us. A propos of nothing he said "don't forget I want to be cremated, (there was no crematorium in Ireland at that time), no tombstone or memorial service, just sprinkle my ashes in the Dublin mountains". Also as he left that evening and after he had kissed me, he said "I think I will go and look at the children before I leave". Four days later he was giving a singing lesson when he had a cerebral haemorrhage and never regained consciousness.

We did as he had asked, he was cremated in Liverpool and we sprinkled his ashes at a favourite place in the Dublin mountains where he and my mother used to picnic. He was very young, 67, and had so much to give. It was a terrible shock at the time but now I am so thankful that he died happy, as my mother did some eleven years later from a heart attack. The Percy Whitehead Cup was later presented to the Feis Ceoil by his pupils in his memory.

OBITUARY

MR. P. WHITEHEAD

The death has taken place in a Dublin hospital of Mr. Percy Whitehead, 29 Castle Park, Rathfarnham, the well-known Dublin singer and teacher. Aged 67, Mr. Whitehead had a long connection with the musical life of Dublin, and during his career earned an outstanding reputation. He was a lifelong friend of the late Count McCormack and of the late Plunket Greene, one of Britain's outstanding singers. Mr. Whitehead had a tremendous influence on the musical life of Dublin, and was responsible for the introduction of many new songs to Ireland. On one occasion he was described by Mr. Greene as the finest interpreter of folk songs in the British Isles.

Mr. Whitehead had the distinction of being one of the earliest broadcasters from the B.B.C., and was also very well known for his work in oratorio. For over 30 years he was a chorister in Christ Church Cathedral, and was a patron of the Culwick Choral Society. In November, 1928, Mr. Whitehead received from the members of the society a present of a mahogany music cabinet. The presentation was made to celebrate the 25th anniversary of his first public appearance as soloist, which took place under the late Dr. J. C. Culwick, founder of the Orpheus Choir. For many years he had been attached to the staff of Alexandra College as a professor of vocal music.

He is survived by his wife, a son and a daughter.

Some years later this letter appeared in the Irish Times in response to an incorrect comment in "An Irishman's Diary".

JOHN McCORMACK

Sir—May I correct a mis-statement in "An Irishman's Diary" (March 24th)? John McCormack never won the Plunkett Greene Cup at Dublin Feis. He won the gold medal in the tenor class in 1903, and shortly after that went abroad. The Plunkett Greene Cup was first won by the late Percy Whitehead in 1908.—Yours, etc.,

W. Egbert Trimble.
The Battery, Enniskillen.
March 24th, 1958.

Newspaper Cutting

My Achilles tendons continued to trouble me but I got by until we were performing in the Empire Pool, Wembley in 1950, celebrating twenty years of the League in England. I felt a very strong pain in my left calf and as I was running off the tendon snapped, at least we had completed our item and I don't think the public were aware that anything had happened. When it healed, the tendon was even shorter. Both tendons continued for many years to limit my movement and to cause me considerable pain.

Invergarry

It soon became apparent to me that the League and my dancing were not very lucrative and I had to do something about it. Having been a bachelor until he was forty years of age Ken found it hard to adapt to family life. I had always been good at and enjoyed knitting, sewing etc. and was making virtually all the children's clothes. A friend and I decided to start a business. I would make children's clothes and she adults, thus was born 'Lindegay', which later became Lindegay Dublin Ltd. Unfortunately we had very different views on customer services and it was not long before I found myself on my own.

I had to have some help with the children so decided to have an 'au pair'. I was very fortunate to find a Swiss girl called Li.

Family with Li

She agreed to come for three months but stayed for fifteen, by which time she had become one of the family. Her Swiss boyfriend, as you can imagine was not happy, so she returned to him but we missed her very much. That was over fifty years ago, but we still keep in touch. I have visited her and her husband and she has two sons and is a grandmother.

With Li in Basle 1999

By then I was dressmaking every spare moment I had, but I was able to do this at home. When I was about forty years old I had a bad injury to my back. When X-rayed I was found to have arthritis nearly everywhere, the prognosis was not good. Anyway I kept exercising and forty-five years later I am still without pain or disability and lead an active life – surely no further proof is needed that "Movement is Life".

After two more 'au pair' girls – one good and one hopeless I was recommended a Dutch girl called Lies, who was in her late twenties, she came for a year but stayed for nearly sixteen. At that time Gillian and Dallas were six and three years respectively so she was with us as they grew up. Also she was able to help me a bit with sewing and embroidery and also with caring for Ken's father who lived with us for some years.

Family with Lies and Crusoe

With Lies in Zwolle, The Netherlands 1976

Dallas with "Bibby" in Ardamine

Snake Charmers !

In 1953 we moved to a big old house in Silchester Road, Glenageary, which we named Invergarry. We got it very reasonably as it was in such poor condition, not having been repaired or decorated since 1909. My mother was horrified when she saw it, but I thought the main front room, which was thirty feet long would be perfect for my classes. Looking back it was a huge undertaking, especially as we never seemed to have any spare money. I continued teaching in Shangrila Hotel, Dalkey and in St. Thomas' in Fosters Avenue.

Front garden Invergarry

Back garden Invergarry

Back garden Invergarry

Shortly after we moved in my Uncle Alfie, Iris and their youngest child Heather visited us. It was a nostalgic trip for him and he visited many of the areas he had known well growing up.

Uncle Alfie and family shortly before his death 1955

Two years later he died leaving a wife and three girls - Mary aged 13, Diana aged 11 and Heather aged 8. To me it was like losing a second father and of course I was so sad for his family. I felt privileged to have been so close to him for years. Iris died towards the end of the twentieth century and sadly Heather lost a battle with cancer in 2002 at the young age of 56. Mary and Diana continue to live in the South of England.

Slowly but surely the house became habitable and after about two years I was able to transfer my classes from the Shangrila Hotel. Invergarry – our new home became very important for the League. The classes grew and eventually I was teaching two mornings, two evenings and one afternoon, the latter being children mainly, with one class for mothers. By then I had stopped teaching in Mount Merrion, but I had adult and children's classes in Kill O' the Grange, in the old Church Hall, - not the best of venues. Now the adult classes thrive there in their lovely new hall at the back of the Church.

In Invergarry I trained nineteen League teachers and over one hundred Extend teachers. The latter training necessitated my taking a special course in England in 1984. Many years earlier one of the English League teachers who had previously been a nurse, saw what a poor quality of life the great majority of older people had, who were living in nursing homes or in geriatric hospitals. She realised that the League had much to offer them, thus Extend was formed. I returned from there and completed the first training in 1985.

Gillian went to Glengara Park School. While there she enjoyed hockey, tennis and swimming. Outside of school she also played tennis and belonged to a swimming club, as well as being a Brownie, Guide and Ranger. She was also developing an interest in a variety of handcrafts.

Dallas attended Kingstown Grammar School, which later merged with Avoca School to become Newpark Comprehensive. He enjoyed both hockey and tennis. Kingstown was co-educational and he had a large circle of friends. They cycled everywhere and I think it is just as well I was unaware of some of their exploits! On one occasion he was caught in a speed trap, while cycling down Lower Glenageary Road, doing 37 m.p.h. in a 30 m.p.h. limit. This caused much amusement but fortunately he wasn't charged.

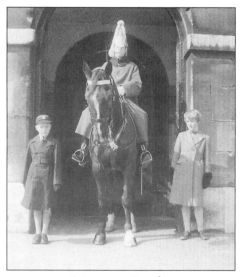

1st visit to London

Both Gillian and Dallas played tennis for many years in Glenageary Tennis Club and Dallas was a ball boy at Fitzwilliam for the Irish Open Championships for some years, this he really enjoyed. Over the years, although I was very busy, I got so much pleasure from following the children's activities and where possible, went to watch matches or to plays, prizegivings etc.

In the early years we holidayed in the coastguard station in Ballymoney, but then I bought a small bungalow in Ardamine, Co. Wexford, which we used as a holiday home. Each summer we, as a family spent August there, my mother used to come with us. The children loved it and had many friends to meet up with on a yearly basis. I personally looked on it as an escape and the chance to renew my energy for the year ahead.

There were families that we met there in the 1950s that we have kept in contact with. Gillian is in regular contact with some of the Furlong family, the Kilroys were friends for many years, the oldest son, Howard, married Meriel McCullagh – no relation, but a daughter of Bob McCullagh who had been one of my father's pupils. The Quigley family still spend their summers there, now the next generation holiday with their children and enjoy boating and water-skiing. They have over the years been very generous in the use of their boats, and have given many children the opportunity to try out water activities. The Fleming family originally travelled from England for the holidays, they then built a permanent house and moved to live in Ardamine, they now run Caravan Parks in the area. The Mackay family always remained friends, Geoff acted as compere for my "This is Your Life"; Jean continues to holiday next door to us in Ardamine; Alan, who was friendly with Dallas during childhood lives in Bray and Gillian is part of a craft group with his wife Heather. Gillian and Dan and their children use the bungalow now.

Gillian and Dallas - Ardamine

With friends including Roger, his mother, Doris, my mother and Lies outside the bungalow in Ardamine

Gillian with Howard Kilroy

The beach at Ardamine

Vanessa

In 1960 Gillian asked me if I would approach Matron in the Cottage Home for Little Children, which was very near where we lived. She was very keen to help in the children's home during her school holidays. Both she and Dallas always loved children and were very good with babies and young children.

She was always talking about one particular baby who was very special to her. As usual I was very busy but delighted that she was enjoying helping. On September 13th, 1960 she arrived home and put this baby on my knee, we looked at each other and it was love at first sight! It turned out to be the baby's first birthday. Anyway I rang Matron and asked if we could take Vanessa (although that was not her name then) out once a week on a regular basis. This was agreed provided it was every week for the sake of the child's security.

The first Sunday I called for her she cried when I collected her, the second Sunday she greeted me by jumping up and down in her cot and cried when I brought her back! Thus began a relationship for life. She was soon coming to us twice a week and then three times. By then I was determined to adopt her but I said nothing to anybody as I had many obstacles to overcome.

Her mother was an Irish nurse and her father an Indian doctor, I think they met when working in England though he trained in the College of Surgeons in Dublin. Her mother's parents put severe pressure on her to give up her baby who was already being cared for in the Cottage Home. Vanessa's father continued to support her and visited her when he could. He was a South African Indian, so it was not possible at that time for him to have a mixed race child in South Africa, nor could he even acknowledge her existence.

At that time it was very rare to see other than white people in Ireland. As a nation we were supposed to be very tolerant and anti-racial. Nothing was further from the truth. The Irish salvaged their conscience by collecting money for 'black babies' as though they were only to be pitied and, of course, inferior. They even boasted of their tolerance until their own son or daughter was in danger of falling in love with a person with the wrong coloured skin. I knew my friends and relations would think me quite mad for taking on more responsibility but that was the least of my problems.

According to the Adoption Society it was considered impossible for a white family to rear a mixed race child. At that time there were so many white babies available for adoption whereas now most mothers keep their babies and parents are only too willing to adopt different race children, and indeed are making a great success of it.

At that time my mother was living with us and also got much pleasure from Vanessa, she used to say that she never knew a baby could have a sense of humour at such a young age. As all bedrooms were occupied I had a bit of a problem there.

After Christmas of that year my mother who thoroughly enjoyed the festivities took to her bed and was too tired to get up. This was so unlike her as she was fiercely independent and had been going to her bridge club each week. Fifteen years previously the Doctor had told her that her blood pressure was so high she was at stroke point. He told her she must give up golf and stop riding her bike. She considered this was no life for her so she ignored him and proved him wrong! Shortly after 9.00 a.m. on 3rd January 1961 she rang her bell to tell me she had a very bad pain in her chest. I called Lies to phone the Doctor, but she was dead in twenty minutes. I was with her at the time and it was then that I realised she had had many minor heart attacks and survived. She used to refer to them as "a bit of a bad turn". She would have been seventy-six the following March.

At 11.00 a.m. that morning I had a phone call from Matron in the Cottage Home to tell me that Vanessa was available for adoption. I explained that my mother had just died and that I would be in touch as soon as possible, as you can imagine she was really embarrassed over her timing. I suppose I am basically a very practical person but this experience dispelled any doubts I might have had as to the feasibility of adopting Vanessa.

When I first mentioned it to the family the children were thrilled and Ken agreed she could live with us but was not prepared

Age 11

Hazel with President Mary Robinson, March 1991, after the laying of the foundation stone for St. Andrew's and Newcourt Schools

My New Zealand friends, Colleen and Max, in Invergarry

With grandchildren in Invergarry - Christmas 1994

With Dallas and my cousin Mary (Uncle Alfie's eldest daughter)

Namibia - Hazel with friend

Mathew at a circus school, Club Med in Noumea

Capetown and Table Mountain

Noumea, New Caledonia

Sand Dunes at Sossusvlei, Namibia

Spitzkoppe Mountain in Namibia

View of the Dargle River from my balcony

Flowers on my balcony

With Dan, Hazel and Adam in Guernsey

Mathew with "Bill", a horse in "Lord of the Rings", in New Zealand

My ballooning experience - New Zealand 2004
(I took this photo from the third balloon)

February 2004 on Kaiteriteri beach (Photo taken by Vanessa)

U.C.D. Golden Jubilee 1984

U.C.D. 1984 Finale with Dorothie and Sarah
(Vanessa in pale green skirt)

The Concert Hall 1989

Albert Hall Finale 1990

Basketball Arena 1994

Basketball Arena 1994 - Finale

Irish Team in Albert Hall 1995

With Irish Team outside Albert Hall 1995 (Gillian 4th from right at back)

Irish Team, Albert Hall 2000 (Gillian under light)

to adopt. The night before her arrival I was busy making nighties and Gillian and Dallas were getting her room ready and Ken suddenly decided we couldn't have her. The children were devastated as I was, but I was also furious. It was a difficult moment, but I won in the end.

As Vanessa had visited us regularly there was no trauma when she came to stay permanently, and she was immediately one of the family. Before her visits to us she was considered a bit backward but after a few visits, Matron could not believe the change in her – all she needed was one to one attention and it wasn't long before she was one step ahead of us all. Physically she was incredibly co-ordinated. While still in her cot and before she could walk she was often found crawling around on the floor. Her method was to get one leg over and drop to the ground. Later on if she fell downstairs she would pick herself up and laugh. She was quite a challenge to look after but very rewarding.

Vanessa's first photo after arrival with us

Vanessa aged 2

We had a high wall round our garden, which was a great temptation to Vanessa, as she grew older. By this time I decided she had to learn the hard way. I heard one of her young friends asking her "does your Mummy let you do that, mine wouldn't". I must admit I felt a bit guilty. Anyway the inevitable happened and Vanessa fell and broke her arm. I was in the garden at the time, I asked her if she was hurt, she said "no" and promptly did a cartwheel to prove it and broke a second bone. She was a born leader and most of her escapades were just high spirits.

She attended Glengara Park School from the age of four following immediately after Gillian who had been there for twelve years.

Dallas and Vanessa at the zoo

From the beginning she knew her background and was remarkably secure considering the problems she encountered as she was growing up. She had a loving home and a reasonably disciplined upbringing, which has always stood to her.

As she once said to me "you didn't just adopt me, I adopted you". I think that about sums it up.

Vanessa age 9 - 1st day water skiing

My three children

In the meantime the children were growing up. Gillian went to train as an Occupational Therapist in Dorset House in Oxford and Dallas opted for the Bank. Gillian came home from college for her 21st birthday, which was celebrated in the Glencormack Hotel, Co. Wicklow (where Avoca Handweavers are now). I had both legs in plaster after my Achilles tendon operation and Ken was very unwell, but had not yet been diagnosed as having leukaemia. All in all her parents were not the best! The only bright spark was Vanessa; she was seven and a half and stayed with Ken at the hotel for the night, while the rest of us went home. Exactly two weeks later the hotel was burnt to the ground.

It was some time before Ken's illness was diagnosed, but eventually he was given at most a year and a half to live. He had almost completed his service in the bank, but he resigned, as he felt unable to go back to work.

He had become very fond of Vanessa so he was keen to adopt. Needless to say we were all delighted. It took months to complete all the formalities. Eventually we were all called to a meeting of the Adoption Board. By then Vanessa was eight years old and she had to attend also, and had to be asked what she thought about the adoption! When asked if she would like us as her Daddy and Mummy, her answer was "I suppose so" – high praise from her! At this stage she could remember no other life.

Tendon Surgery

Over the years every effort was made to avoid surgery on my Achilles tendons, even having them both lengthened under anaesthetic and then my legs put in plaster – all to no avail. Finally after seventeen years I had both tendons surgically lengthened by Boyd Dunlop, an orthopaedic surgeon. I had known him for many years and his wife, Evelyn, was one of my father's pupils and an important member of his choir. At that time it was not an operation to be taken lightly, especially as I was nearing fifty years of age. Now it is commonplace and if done on young children, the recovery is very fast but it continues to be an athlete's nightmare when they have recurring problems with their Achilles tendons.

Because I had both tendons lengthened at the same time, I had to spend four weeks in bed in St. Michael's Nursing Home (no longer open). I had arranged with Boyd Dunlop to have the operation as soon after Christmas as possible so that I wouldn't have to miss too much of the new League term. As I had a private room I was able to conduct Lindegay business once I had got through the pain and trauma of the operation.

I was not ill as such, so the nurses spent some of their free time with me and I have to admit I enjoyed my stay there, in many ways it was an escape from my very pressurised life at the time. Added to which in the next room was a friend, Arthur Spence, who had a great sense of humour and we shared many a joke.

Most of the time I had the use of a phone so was able to keep in touch with my customers. Gillian and Dallas collected from my workers, I sorted the knitwear and at times I had quite a few boxes under the bed, I am sure I wouldn't get away with that now! One day Dallas came to tell me that a box of knitwear had been stolen from the car, he was very upset about it. Some three days later the box was found thrown in a hedge in the Pavilion Cinema grounds, it was intact and fortunately it had not rained. I can imagine the thief was somewhat disappointed when he found only baby knitwear.

As I was immobile for so long I was very aware that my muscle tone would deteriorate very quickly so I regularly exercised the rest of my body, in some cases using isometrics. This was always early in the morning and helped me to fill in the time until breakfast.

Once a week there was communion for patients who wished to take part, if they did not wish it, their room door was closed. One of these mornings I was exercising as usual and was doing a shoulder stand in the bed with my two plastered legs in the air.

In walked Reverend Mother and a Priest. Well, I never saw a quicker exit! Apparently this was seen by some of the staff including the nurse who should have closed my door. She thought I would be very annoyed, but when she saw I was amused, she and her companions had a good laugh. To this day I never knew that news could travel so fast. There was a meeting in Dublin that night, which I would normally have attended and this episode was a talking point there.

On a more serious note, when I first was allowed up and had walking plasters, I had no difficulty getting around – first with

As seen in hospital

crutches and then without and never had a problem with balance. I used to go shopping without crutches; in fact I rarely used them. In retrospect it was probably not a good idea as it put enormous pressure on my heels. I taught even with both legs in plaster, in fact it was much harder once I came out of the plaster.

Still teaching after leg surgery

There were times when I wondered if I had gone from the frying pan into the fire. It took a good year for me to recover fully. Since then I have had no problems with my legs or feet.

In January 1968 Gillian went to Canada with a college friend (who is still living there), to get some postgraduate experience in a Children's Rehabilitation centre in St. John's, Newfoundland. They then travelled around North America for two months on Greyhound buses, covering 20,000 miles and had a great time.

At the same time Ken went to stay with his sister and family in Rhodesia (as Zimbabwe was known then). The climate suited him and he had a good remission, so much so that he went to the Mexico Olympics in 1968 as manager of the Irish swimming team. Gillian had arranged to come home because of his illness, she travelled by ship which took a week but she really enjoyed the trip. In the meantime he had arranged to go to Mexico; he went by air, so in fact passed her somewhere over the Atlantic!

Invergarry garden 1969 after leg surgery

When Vanessa was about 10 years old I had a friend staying with me who became ill. I was advised by the Doctor to get her back to her home in Holland immediately. Ken rang a friend who was an official at the airport to arrange tickets; I got my passport out to discover it expired that very day. I phoned my friend's brother to ask him to meet us at Schipol airport, which is quite some way from where he lived. He spoke very little English and I spoke even less Dutch but I hoped he understood. I duly arrived at Dublin airport, got her out of the car, collected tickets and was helped to get her on board.

When Vanessa got home from school, she asked Ken where I was, he said – "she's in Holland", Vanessa replied "don't be silly Daddy, where is she?" She took quite some convincing. We arrived safely in Holland and were met. I, of course, could not leave the airport, as I had to return while my passport was still valid.

Suddenly I realised that I had left the car at the only entrance to the one small airport building in Dublin. This is hard to visualise, considering the size of Dublin airport now. I took the next available flight back to London and phoned Ken to tell him what I had done. He already knew as the police had been on to him, they thought they were dealing with a stolen car. He told me to go to an official at Dublin Airport to collect the keys of the car, which had been put in the car park.

I arrived in Dublin in the middle of the night – not an official to be seen and no information as to where to find the car. As luck would have it, for once, I had spare keys in my bag; I eventually found the car and arrived home safely but totally exhausted. It took me weeks to recover! I never even got a parking summons – changed times, I probably was classified as mad!!

In the end Ken lived for three and a half years instead of his prognosis of one and a half years. Towards the end he had great companionship and pleasure from Vanessa.

He died in St. Luke's Hospital, aged 67; he gave his body to medical science and we had a special service some days later.

Vanessa was still at Glengara but a year later she was accepted for Masonic Girls School which in turn closed after a year, as there were so few pupils. She transferred to Drogheda Grammar School as a boarder where she was very happy. She did very well academically but also excelled in athletics, particularly the triple jump, which unfortunately in those days was not a women's event, so she got no opportunity to continue with it after she left school.

From there she went to Trinity where she studied Marine Biology and took the Higher Diploma of Education. She loved Trinity and felt very privileged to have had the opportunity to study there.

During her latter school years and early college years, she worked for The Duke of Edinburgh award, achieving the Silver in 1976 and the gold in 1979. To receive the gold award, she and I were invited to Buckingham Palace where Vanessa received her award from the Duke of Edinburgh.

We were very fortunate as it was televised in the throne room for the first time. All the young people had a chance to sit on the throne before His Royal Highness arrived. A virtually then unknown Gloria Hunniford was in charge of the media. The whole visit was very informal. The grand staircase was very imposing but all very

Vanessa—our own Gold Medal girl

A YOUNG southside girl was awarded the Duke of Edinburgh Gold Medal last week.

She is 20-year-old Vanessa McCullagh from Glenageary and Prince Philip presented her with the medal at a ceremony in the Throne Room of Buckingham Palace.

The award is made to young people from Ireland, Britain, and British Commonwealth countries who successfully complete a number of courses ranging from mountaineering and various sports, to community work.

In 1976, Vanessa received the Silver Medal for her part in saving the life of a companion who became ill during a hiking trip in the Mourne Mountains.

She crawled into a sleeping bag with the sick girl to keep her warm while two others went for help.

But it was the wide variety of Vanessa's other interests and activities which made her eligible for the Gold Medal award.

In badminton, hockey, long jumping and sprinting she reached the levels of excellence demanded by the committee which gives the awards.

And while a pupil at Drogheda Grammar School she worked for a year with old people and helped in a scheme for holidays for children.

Vanessa, who is now a student at Trinity

College was the only person from the Republic of Ireland amongst 800 young people who received their awards last week.

"The palace was very beautiful," said Vanessa. "We were in the Throne Room where the walls were painted white, but a lot of the plaster has gold on it. There were cases containing silver – and even the loos had mahogany seats!."

"It was very nice to get the award because I love sports and doing lots of different things. Perhaps one day it may help me get a job teaching other children to enjoy what gave me so much pleasure," she said.

Newspaper Cutting 14/11/79

Vanessa's graduation

simply decorated. The corridors were lined with portraits of the Queen's ancestors and we even had a peep at the ballroom. All in all a great day, finishing with a visit to the theatre to see 'Evita'.

After Vanessa finished college, she and her friend Sandra Rooney went to work in the U.S.A. They were prepared to do any job. When they had enough money saved they bought an old camper van and set off across the States, Vanessa did all the driving, they couldn't even lock their door. However they survived and eventually reached San Francisco. By then the van was falling apart and they were virtually penniless. I am not sure what Sandra did but Vanessa did a bar tenders course which gave her the entrée to quite lucrative work. Eventually they returned home and I for one was very relieved. As Vanessa now admits, she wouldn't like to do it now!

Photo of Vanessa which was used in the English League Diary

With Pharaoh

The Next Generation

In 1979 Dallas married Stella Carmody. Their daughter Sarah was born in August 1980 and their son Kenneth in February 1983.

Dallas's Wedding

Sarah's Christening

Dallas, Vanessa & Sarah

Sarah

Kenneth smelling the roses

*Kenneth & Sarah in
Dan & Gillian's garden*

Sarah with her pony Patch

*Kenneth on bar
Invergarry*

Sarah & Pippa

Gillian married Dan Buckley in 1980, their daughter Hazel was born in August 1985 and their son Adam in June 1988, just as I first became ill with cancer.

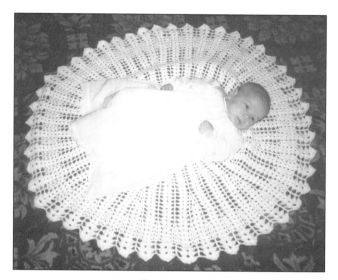

Hazel's Christening

Sarah with Hazel 1985

Gillian, Sarah, Kenneth, Hazel & Adam - Howth

Hazel with Adam

Dan, Hazel and Sandy

Having a nap - Adam & Pharaoh

*My 50 years teaching
with Hazel*

The Buckley family in France

*Gillian with Adam
looking at Hazel's photo
in the magazine*

Adam with Shadow

Hazel and Adam outside the bungalow in Ardamine

Gillian and Adam painting

Hazel

Vanessa and Christophe Rey went to New Caledonia – originally for 2 years, in August 1987. David was born in March 1990 and Mathew in September 1991. They still live there.

Vanessa and David

*Vanessa & boys 1991
Killiney Hill*

Vanessa with David and Mathew - New Caledonia 1992

With David and Mathew - Noumea

Vanessa and boys - Noumea

With David and Mathew - Noumea

David - Noumea

David and Mathew - Noumea

Catamaran trip with Christophe and the boys

Three Generations - What a likeness!

Isolde   *Gillian*   *Hazel*

Three Generations 1994

Grandchildren on Invergarry stairs 1994

David, Hazel, Mathew and Adam in Noumea

Having grown up with Kerry Blue Terriers, it was not long after I was married that I acquired a Kerry Blue pup that grew into a very handsome dog that we called Bomber. We then had his daughter, Raffles, followed by her son Crusoe. Next I had a black poodle called Kim, following his death I returned to having a Kerry Blue called Pharaoh who died in 1992 while I was in Noumea with Vanessa. It was six months later that I had the courage to replace him with a West Highland Terrier called Pippa. She has been a great joy to me and very companionable, especially now that I live on my own in an apartment. She is now 11 years old and I try not to think too far ahead.

Bomber

Pippa

Extend Ireland

Extend is a system of exercises to music, based on the League principles, which aims to enhance the quality of life, improving posture, health, vitality and mobility. It is designed as a recreational activity for older men and women and for less able people of all ages. It is mostly done sitting on chairs. It is also of benefit to people with such problems as Autism, various forms of brain damage, Alzheimer's, Multiple Sclerosis and Parkinson's.

*Extend (Miriam working with a parachute in Day Cemtre
for people with Alzheimer's*

The training for this work is shorter than the League training but many teachers already have a paramedical background or Physical Education. Many teach in Nursing Homes and their sessions are looked forward to from week to week. It brings together movement, exercise and music and provides interest, stimulation and fun. It is also very much a group activity, unlike so many other exercise regimes. It can provide one of the situations where interaction with others becomes a valuable part of the resident's day.

The following appreciation was written by Joan Kealy, when she was Senior Physiotherapist in the Day Hospital in St. James's.

"EXTEND" is exercise to music for the elderly and disabled and it was started in this country in 1984 by Isolde McCullagh. The exercises are designed to keep our ageing population as active as possible, so that they may keep whatever mobility they have and be able to enjoy life to the full. I first met Isolde when our Special Interest Group invited her to demonstrate her work as Tutor and Development Training Officer for "Extend". I found her demonstration to be the most exciting demonstration I had seen in a long time and I felt that I wanted to be able to emulate her. In my capacity as Senior Physiotherapist in the Department of Medicine for the Elderly in St. James's Hospital, I wanted to learn how to enhance the value of our daily exercise groups and make them more beneficial and enjoyable. The opportunity to learn presented itself in 1989 when an "EXTEND" course was held. Myself and another physiotherapist and three occupational therapists from St. James's attended the course and were most impressed. As a result, Isolde was invited to demonstrate her techniques to the medical, nursing and physiotherapy staffs in St. James's. The attendance at her demonstration was three times the number that usually attend such sessions. (We had no platform on which she could perform so she called for a table, leaped on to it and demonstrated on the table where everyone could see her! !). It was a marvellous performance. The result of all this is that Isolde's exercises are now being used daily in St. James's Hospital both by physiotherapists and occupational therapists. Patients look forward to the morning and afternoon exercise which have been most successful and enjoyable. Isolde McCullagh is a very special person and we are most fortunate in our time to have the benefit of her skill, experience and above all enthusiasm.

Long may she thrive.

Joan Kealy

At first I held one course a year but demand made it necessary to do more, also we needed to spread the work throughout Ireland. Though Dublin and surrounding counties have the most Extend teachers we have now run courses in Cork, Galway, Castlebar and Kilkenny and hopefully will increase this trend in the coming years. During the early courses I asked Seona Ross, an experienced Extend teacher, over from England to share some of her ideas with us.

In November 1997, Betty O'Donoghue, a South African teacher of long standing, came all the way to us to train both as an Extend teacher and a tutor. This proved a great success; we enjoyed having her as much as she enjoyed being with us.

I have the greatest admiration for so many of our Extend teachers who need great patience, initiative, dedication and devotion for this specialised work and I know they find it very rewarding even though it is very hard work.

To quote Richard Asher in 1947

> *"Teach us to live that we may dread*
> *Unnecessary time in bed*
> *Get people up and we may save*
> *Our patients from an early grave".*

What was superbly stated in 1947 is even more relevant today.

The following quotations are read to all Extend teachers at the completion of their course.

Beatitudes for the Aged — Anon

> *Blessed are they who understand*
> *My faltering step and palsied hand.*
> *Blessed are they who seem to know*
> *My eyes are dim and wits are slow.*
> *Blessed are they who looked away*
> *When coffee was spilt on the table today.*
> *Blessed are they with a cheery smile*
> *Who stop to chat for a little while.*
> *Blessed are they who never say*
> *"You've told that story twice today".*
> *Blessed are they who know the way*
> *To bring back memories of yesterday.*

Blessed are they who make it known
I'm loved, respected, and not alone
Blessed are they who ease the days
On my journey home in loving ways.

"Please Do See Me"

"As thy days, so shall thy strength be" - Deuteronomy 33 : 25

What do you see, Nurse, what do you see?
What are you thinking when you look at me ?
A crabbit old woman, not very wise,
Uncertain of habit, with faraway eyes
Who dribbles her food and makes no reply
When you say in a loud voice "I do wish you'd try ".
Who seems not to notice the things that you do
And forever is losing a sock or a shoe.
Who, unresisting, lets you do as you will.
With bathing and feeding the long day to fill.
Is that what you're thinking, is that what you see?
Then open your eyes, Nurse, you're not looking at ME.

I'll tell you who I am as I sit here so still,
As I ease at your bidding and eat at your will.
I'm a small child of ten with a father and mother,
Brothers and sisters who love one another:
A young girl of sixteen with wings on her feet,
Dreaming that soon now a lover she'll meet.
A bride soon at twenty - my heart gives a leap
Remembering the vows that I promised to keep.
At twenty - five now I have young of my own
Who need me to build a secure happy home.
A woman of thirty, my young now grow fast,
Bound to each other with ties that should last.
At forty my young sons are grown and are gone,
But my man is beside me to see I don't mourn.
At fifty once more babies play round my knee.
Again we know children, my loved one and me.

Dark days are upon me, my husband is dead.
The years once so joyful, how quickly they sped.
My young are all rearing young ones of their own,
And I think of the years and the love I have known.
I'm an old woman now and nature is cruel.
Her jest is to make old age look like a fool.
The body it crumbles, grace and vigour depart,
Now there's a stone where I once had a heart.
But inside this old carcass a young girl still dwells,
And now and again my battered heart swells.
I remember the joys, I remember the pain,
And I'm loving and living life over again.
I think of the years, all too few - gone too fast,
And accept the stark fact that nothing can last.
So open your eyes, Nurse, open and see
Not a crabbit old woman - "LOOK CLOSER - SEE ME !"

Lindegay Dublin Ltd.

While this was all happening I was developing my business. At one stage I was personally making all the school summer dresses for the Hall School, Monkstown, later to be amalgamated with Hillcourt and Park House Schools, to become Rathdown; it later was joined by Glengara Park. They were all separate schools when I was making the summer uniforms. Pims of South Great George's Street, Dublin were the uniform suppliers. I also became quite well known for children's smocked dresses, which I made for private customers. Looking back I wonder if I ever slept, not surprising that I need very little sleep even now when I could have as much as I want! It gradually occurred to me that I was giving a good service for very little reward.

I always knitted my own children's jumpers and also Gillian's Swiss socks. I advertised for knitters to knit the socks and got three suitable replies, these knitters worked for me for years, but, as in all handwork, it can never be adequately rewarded, it has to be a labour of love.

Over the years I gradually reduced the dressmaking and increased the number of knitters. By the late 1960s I had knitters all over the country, also finishers and embroideresses and had totally stopped the dressmaking. The next step was to approach the retailers. I started with Walpole's in Suffolk Street, probably at that time the most prestigious and expensive shop in Dublin. I approached the buyer, I can't remember her name but she terrified me and criticised everything but gave me an order. I spent a sleepless night wondering how on earth I was going to fulfil the order, at this stage I was concentrating on socks and baby knitwear. Anyway I managed it and in a few years was supplying Brown Thomas' and Newell's in Grafton Street as well, also Arnott's in Henry Street. Newell's buyer left and opened her own shop in Wicklow Street and I supplied her.

A Hobby that became a Business

THERE'S a sign or placard affixed to the front doors of the building from which this writing emananates which says "Linde Gay". We've passed the sign hundreds of times but, as these things sometimes are, it had achieved the anonymity of the familiar.

Until last week, when we came face to face with Mrs. Isolde McCullagh, inventor and perpetrator of the title.

She is a daughter of the late Percy Whitehead, and is by calling physical training instructress and a housewife. And more. She always loved wool and knitting

Employs Eighty Knitters

She started about ten years ago, now employs 80 knitters around the country, supplies the larger firms in Dublin as well as Harrods in London and stores in America with children's wear.

The name 'Linde Gay' has no family connotations. "We were looking for a name that would suggest children's wear. We thought of 'Linde' — and then 'Gay' just happened."

Mrs. McCullagh conducts the whole business herself from a not-oversize store-cum-office, has never had to look for buyers—apart from Harrods, where she "just went in and asked for the buyer."

Irish Swimming Champion

Apart from the business she teaches physical culture in her own home in Glenageary to classes "ranging from two-year-olds to I won't say what age". She's a member of the York Road Dramatic Society. She was quarter mile Irish swimming champion, calls the standard of this sport in Ireland "appalling".

"We lack proper facilities. They're really the worst in the world—especially for all-the-year-round training. And especially for divers. There are no boards in Tara Street for winter-training."

This week the McCullagh family, two children, mother and father, are by the sea in Wexford

MRS. ISOLDE McCULLAGH

where every August they "retire into private life."

Happy thought.

Lindegay article 19/8/1960 - Pillar Post - Lelia Doolan

Once I was satisfied that I could safely supply the demand in Dublin I decided to try London. I had an aunt by marriage living there, although we were actually the same age; she was married to my much-loved Uncle Alfie, who had looked after me when I was training in London. We became good friends.

Iris and I went to all the well-known shops such as John Lewis, Selfridges and Debenhams without any success. It wasn't a question of their not being interested in what I had to offer, they wouldn't even see me without an appointment and sometimes that was weeks ahead. By this time I had virtually given up when Iris said to me "Why don't we start at the top, let's go to Harrod's". Thus began a wonderful business relationship; I first supplied the baby department, the buyer recommended me to the Toddler buyer and so on until I was supplying them from baby to teens.

I designed all the knitwear myself, years earlier I had been shown how to do Swiss darning which is a form of embroidery put on after the jumper is knitted. I think I was one of the first manufacturers to have motifs on plain knitwear. This was a huge success, the most popular designs were a horse's head, skier, soldier, stag's head etc. and for the babies – rabbits and Scotty dogs.

By this time Lindegay had become a family business with Gillian and Lies doing embroidery and Dallas folding and bagging. There was also a constant need for work to be collected from knitters and finishers. From Thursday afternoon to Tuesday afternoon I had the table tennis table up in my front room studio and used it for sorting the knitwear. Come Tuesday, everything had to be boxed and put away ready for my classes on Tuesdays, Wednesdays and Thursdays. My League members got used to seeing boxes piled up in the hall.

Frequently when Gillian or Dallas went anywhere by car, there was bound to be a knitter or finisher to be delivered to or collected from. This was a condition of borrowing my car!

The Irish Export Board (then Córas Trachtála) put me in touch with an American buyer, but he was only interested in large quantities using a cheaper yarn, this I was not prepared to do. He in turn introduced me to Lilly Rauglas – the children's buyer from Bergdorf Goodman. I met her in the Shelbourne Hotel and she was immediately interested.

Outside White House after meeting President Kennedy, just three weeks before he was assassinated. I am extreme right of photo.

When President Kennedy visited Ireland he invited a group of exporters, of which I was one, to visit the White House. Needless to say we didn't need a second invitation. I arranged to meet Lilly at Berdorf Goodman's the morning after we arrived in New York. I did not know that she had resigned and was leaving that day but she asked could she be my agent. Obviously I was delighted but, at the same time, a bit scared in case I wouldn't be able to cope with the orders. I was aware that the Irish had a very bad reputation for not fulfilling orders on time, and indeed had witnessed overenthusiastic manufacturers promising what even I realised was impossible. I was determined not to fall into that trap.

There were many events organised for us including our trip to the White House, the latter was quite an experience, the President met us on the lawn outside the Oval Office. He was very friendly and we all took lots of photos. Three weeks later he was assassinated and I really felt it as a personal loss. Like everybody else I know exactly where I was and what I was doing when I heard the news.

Vanessa modelling Lindegay knitwear

In the right, a handknit cabled jacket in scarlet. Left, a two-colour jersey available in a variety of shades.

A selection of handknit sweaters for boys and girls.

Quality is what sells the hand-knitted children's woollies produced by "Lindegay, Dublin." Started about ten years ago with three knitters, to-day there are one hundred on the pay roll. "I love working with wool, and it began when my children were young and I knitted for them," said Mrs. Isolde McCullagh, whose hobby has developed into an industry. She insists on a high standard of knitting and finish, and discerning buyers were soon clamouring for this most attractive children's knitwear. Lindegay socks, she told me, ankle or knee-length, hand-knitted in interesting stitches, have become one of her most popular lines, so popular she can't get her knitters to turn them off their needles fast enough.

In Dublin you'll find the Lindegay label on woollies from layette stage to teenage stage (not forgetting V-neck and crew necks and shawl collars for the boys) at Arnott's, Brown Thomas, Newells and Walpoles. You'll come across them, too, in Harrods of London, and Rackmans of Birmingham, one of the finest stores in Europe, I'm told. In the U.S.A.,

Bergdorf Goodman and Lord and Taylor have them, while in San Francisco they're at Ashbrook's.

Newspaper Cutting - The Irish Times - 10/7/1963
A Touch of Luxury by Ida Grehan

From the business point of view the trip was a great success for me, though at the time I had no idea how it would go. Eventually I was supplying many of the well know superior stores in the States but all through Lilly, which was ideal for me. Though quite a lot of the business was baby wear I found it very different from the Irish and British trade. Here it was still very much geared to little girls being little girls and boys little boys. In the States the babies were born old! I found myself supplying sweaters for the new born in the colour of the university attended by one or both of their parents, e.g. a large white 'H' embroidered on maroon for Harvard and a white 'Y' on royal blue for Yale. These jumpers (as we called them) were ordered from the baby sizes up to teens. I came to know so many of the American Universities and their colours, but business thrived.

Mrs. Kevin McClory (Bobo Sigrist) at Dublin Airport.
Children wearing Lindegay socks. (Photo from the Irish Times)

As a result I constantly needed more knitters and finishers. I advertised nationwide which necessitated travelling round Ireland to interview the applicants. At that time Aran Sweaters were becoming very big sellers and most knitters preferred this work, as the wool was thick and the needles big. My trade was entirely different as I used finer wool and sometimes courtelle.

In the late 1960s I had met Betty Higgins through amateur dramatics and we had become very friendly. At that time she was working for a Caravan manufacturer, the business was in trouble and I was persuaded to help financially and became a Director. Unfortunately I joined a sinking ship, the firm collapsed, Betty was out of a job and I was left with 5 caravans and nowhere to put them, more about all this later. Betty became receptionist for the League classes and my part-time secretary in Lindegay.

"Sit Down a Minute Adrian" (me on left)

Cast of "Sit Down a Minute Adrian" (me 3rd from right, back row)

Me as Reverend Mother in "Bonaventure"!

Betty and I used to set off at weekends towing a small caravan so that I could visit new, potential knitters. I did the driving; she did the navigating (not my strong point!). We had some hilarious situations usually when asking for directions to some out of the way farm. One always sticks in my mind. We were looking for a place called Killina; we had the emphasis on the middle syllable and pronounced it as the letter 'i', after much scratching of his head the local we had asked, said, "Aah, you mean Killiná". Well now you go up that road and you will see a Church on your left, but take no notice of that, go on about a mile and you will come to O'Flaherty's bar but take no notice of that". By then we were both becoming pretty hysterical so we decided to battle on and hope for better directions. Before we reached our destination we were given a third pronunciation, but we made it eventually. Having somebody to share these journeys made such a difference as we turned what would have been a nightmare into a good laugh. From these journeys I did get some wonderful workers, but I also had some disasters such as knitwear smelling strongly of turf, or cat's hairs knitted in.

I also had the odd worker who used far more wool than others, it took me a while to realise where my profit was going.

About the middle of the 1970s I felt that Lindegay was becoming more and more difficult from the expansion point of view. There were many reasons for this. Firstly most of my knitters were the older generation when they started working for me and as a result I was losing them because of their inability to continue or indeed in some cases their death.

The price of wool was steadily rising mainly because of the demand for it by the Japanese. Postage was becoming prohibitive and it was essential to my business. I had built up a very personal relationship with most of my workers so I decided to let the business run down by natural wastage. Indeed I had a few sock knitters still supplying me after I ceased trading and I hadn't the heart to stop them. I even still have a few pairs of socks left. The remainder of my wool I now use for knitting blankets for Oxfam so nothing is wasted. People were surprised I didn't sell it as a going concern, but I had no desire to do this.

Lakelands Caravan Park

Returning to my involvement with caravans, having acquired 5 of them I decided to park them in a Caravan Park in Ardamine, Co. Wexford close to where we had our bungalow.

In June 1969 Betty and I picnicked by a small lake in Co. Cavan, what brought us there I have no idea. Afterwards we went for a drive and saw a Caravan Park on the shores of Lough Sillan, Shercock. At that time it had a couple of caravans and two old railway carriages on it but the situation was beautiful and I thought just the spot for our own caravans.

Shercock Caravan Park before alterations

My cousin-in-law Kathleen Kinsey who lived in Bristol had already financed the acquisition of the caravans and agreed to buy the Park provided I was prepared to run it – this I did for 19 years! As I was determined to get Bórd Fáilte recognition the whole area had to be reconstructed, a proper toilet block built and hard standings for the caravans. The railway carriages had to be removed and I still shudder when I think of them swaying in the air, supported only by a comparatively frail looking sling. Once outside the Park a tractor pulled them up the slipway. At times the front of the tractor was off the ground coping with the strain. I have always regretted that I did not have a camera to record it all. As you can imagine all the local people were watching and no doubt thought these Dublin women were quite mad.

For a long time we were looked on almost as foreigners and certainly eccentric! We were always referred to as the ladies from Dublin. We managed to buy an extra piece of land for a camping area. Meanwhile we took in touring caravans but our timing was very bad as the troubles in the North had started and most of the trade had come from there. Also people from other parts of Ireland felt we were too close to the border and so would not travel in a northerly direction.

Still we continued to develop, we got some Bórd Fáilte grants, but there were very few in that organisation who knew any more than we did about caravan parks and I had constant arguments over some of their demands, e.g. hard standing for tents; where you put the tent pegs hadn't occurred to them!

I towed each of the caravans from Wexford to Shercock. The hill out of Navan was a nightmare especially with the 20 foot and 22 foot vans. I just prayed I wouldn't have to stop halfway as I knew I would never get up the rest of the way. All this took about a year to complete and we officially opened on 27th July 1970 including, our shop at the entrance. We were not present because I got word that Ken had died so I returned to Dublin immediately. It never occurred to me to alter the Shercock arrangements as there were others there to supervise. I heard afterwards that people were shocked that the park was not closed. To me it was a private family matter and I would have considered it wrong to inconvenience anybody. Just as when my father died, I took part in a League show before he was a week dead, because I would have let so many people down if I had not attended. That is the way I was brought up and I agree with it, but people are entitled to their own opinions.

We acquired some rowing boats and hired them out. I organised a number of Water Sport Events but I was nearly always unlucky with the weather.

Lakelands Caravan Park, Shercock

We equipped a section of the public land beside the park with playground equipment; this was a great attraction and of course brought business to our shop. Also the town had an annual regatta on the lake and a dance in a marquee beside us. This again meant a lot of hard work and long hours and I usually drove to Dublin in the small hours of Sunday morning on my own. I doubt if I would do it now. But for the fact that we had Rory and Jo Stewart – a local couple as our managers I could never have coped. Later on, as their children grew, they too became involved.

Mobile Home Lakelands, Shercock

Through all this the League and Lindegay were growing apace.

I had for some time been encouraging the social side of the League and we had a few memorable weekends at the Park with League members and their families with a dinner on the Saturday night in Cabra Castle Hotel in Kingscourt. They were a great success but pretty exhausting for me. Like everything else weather played a big part and we weren't always lucky.

I have to admit that over the 19 years that I ran the Park it became an ever-increasing burden because of my other commitments and the need for me to be in three places at once!

Returning from "secret lake" at Shercock

The League
Late 1970s – 1980s

At this stage Kathleen O'Rourke's health was declining though at the time we were all unaware that it was the beginning of Alzheimer's. She was fully aware sometimes that she had a problem but this made it even harder for her. In 1970 she was trying to train three students, but Dorothie and I were unofficially helping. This was very difficult especially for the students.

From this group emerged Shirley Varian. She was already a Remedial Gymnast. Through the years in which I trained nineteen students for the League and over a hundred for Extend, she taught Anatomy and Physiology to them all, the League and Extend owe her a great deal. Though she no longer lectures she remains devoted to the League and its work and is always available for advice. She continues to teach six Extend classes weekly.

In 1974, when the League was 40 years in Ireland I organized a demonstration in the Shelbourne Hotel; it was really to honour Kathleen. As usual Prunella came from London to support us and it was a very happy occasion.

Demonstration in Shelbourne Hotel 1974
to honour Kathleen's 40 years

Pat, Isolde, Kathleen, Prunella, Rhona, Dorothie, Shirley - 1974

Overseas News

IRELAND

Ireland's League of Health, which was founded in Dublin in 1934 by Kathleen O'Rourke, celebrated its fortieth Anniversary on October 26th. An afternoon meeting at the Shelbourne Hotel drew around 400 people.

The Irish members went through their Bagot-Stack sequences under Isolde McCullagh, children aged from 2 to 10 gave a delightful performance under Dorothie Malone, (the tiny tots stealing the show as usual), members had a class from Prunella, and visitors were persuaded to join in with one taken by Pat Rowlandson.

Professor Eithne Gaffney, a League member and a professor in the Royal College of Surgeons, paid tribute to Kathleen for her work in Dublin, which includes starting the Dublin College of Physical Education, and running it from 1944 to 1955, and founding (with Lady Valerie Goulding), the Central Remedial Clinic which has given treatment to thousands of remedial patients. Kathleen is still a Governor of the Clinic.

The evening dinner, attended by over 200, had the warmth and gaiety traditionally associated with Ireland. Harry Booker, husband of Associate Teacher Rhona, was an excellent Master of Ceremonies; Ralph Walker, former Chairman of the *Irish Times*, Prunella, and Pat spoke. Kathleen thanked the members for the many lovely presents given to her, one being a beautiful new facsimile edition of the Book of Kells.

Dublin has classes in five centres in the city and suburbs, and three new Associate Teachers in addition to the Irish teachers trained by Kathleen. Isolde and Dorothie, senior Teachers of the group, did much to help make the 40th Anniversary such a striking success.

Cutting 1974

'This Is Your Life' was the surprise of her life!

Geoff Mackay presents Isolde McCullagh with her "This is Your Life" book

A 'This Is Your Life' show was the surprise of her life for Glenageary woman Isolde McCullagh — for she was its subject.

Over 200 members of the League of Health, from all parts of South County Dublin crowded into the hall at the rear of the Presbyterian Church, York Road, Dun Laoghaire last week to surprise Isolde (60).

Newspaper Cutting

In 1979 I was forty years teaching and I was totally unaware that my members were organising a "This is your Life" evening. My friend Betty organised the programme and Geoff Mackay became Eamon Andrews for the evening. Messages had been sent from friends and colleagues from around the world. Two well-known

The presentation was organised by past and present members of the league, to commemorate Isolde's 40 years as a teacher of physical health. It was a double celebration in many ways, as Isolde also started the Dun Laoghaire Centre of the League of Health, again 40 years ago.

Members of the audience, aged from 2½ to 80 gave Isolde a rousing cheer, as she stepped blinking, into the suddenly brilliantly lit hall, to be met by Mr. Geoff Mackay, who acted as presenter during the evening.

It took many months work to organise the event, contacting schoolmates of Isolde who now live in Australia, people with whom she did her original training for the League of Health and who are now in Canada, and generally researching her background and early days as a trainee and teacher.

Betty Higgins, of Glenageary was the prime motivator of the 'This Is Your Life' presentation.

"The idea was first mooted in November, but after Christmas the pace hotted up. I've been going hammer and tongs at the organisation of the **presentation** since January," said Betty.

Newspaper Cuttings
This Is Your Life
continued

"I was so delighted that everything went according to plan and that the 'veil of secrecy' under which we planned the presentation was not lifted. I'm very grateful to all the members — both past and present who, helped, by their generosity, to make the evening such a resounding success for Isolde," she added.

A visibly moved Isolde commented: "It was fantastic. I was overcome about the whole thing. They even found people from my early days as a teacher."

"It was a night I will remember for the rest of my life, particularly having my family as well as the members of the league at the presentation made it all the more special for me."

Isolde McCullagh originally joined the League as a member in 1937.

She trained in London, starting in 1938, but the war interrupted her studies, so she returned to Dublin to finish her course.

The course was not easy as it included dancing, mime, voice production. Isolde even did a first year medical course at Trinity College, Dublin, before she received her diploma and commenced teaching.

The league is associated with the Women's League of Health and Beauty in England, and at present, plans are well underway to stage a massive 50th anniversary celebration of the league's worldwide existence in the Albert Hall, London, in March.

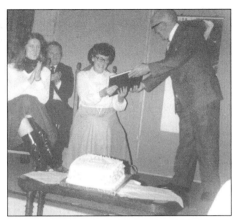

Geoff Mackay presents "This Is Your Life" - 40 years

Dublin businessmen, Roger Percival (seen at back of above photo, behind Stella) and Adrian Jones, were introduced as they had been in my early toddler's class. All in all it was a wonderful evening which I greatly appreciated.

Roger's mother, Doris, is on the right of above photo presenting me with a canteen of cutlery. She was my receptionist for my League classes for some years and a great friend.

Kathleen died in 1980, so I became officially Principal. She was inspired by Mrs. Stack's vision of health and friendship for all and I in turn was inspired by her. Our motto "Movement is Life" was right for the 1930s and is still so right today.

Logo

League Fund Raising

The League has never been in the business of making great profits so once I had it organised on a business footing I felt we should try to support worthy charities. Our first venture was to raise £3000, which was the amount, needed then to train a guide dog for a blind person. In 1882 we had a ten-hour exercise marathon and a public raffle. In all we raised over £7000 so we were able to help a number of worthy causes.

Since then we have supported 27 charitable organisations. During 2002/2003 we raised €12,000 to sponsor the Estonian team, so that they could take part in the Special Olympics which were held in Ireland. In 2003/2004 our project is to raise money for the Children's Hospital, Crumlin. Over the years in excess of €80,000 has been raised.

Marathon 1982

Marathon 1982

Presentation to Special Olympics 2003
The League of Health sponsored Estonia

League's Golden Jubilee

At the time of the marathon I had hand picked from my members three whom I felt would make good teachers. They were Vivienne, Mary and Joan, Vivienne and Mary are now tutors as well as having their own classes, Joan taught for many years and has now retired with her husband to Spain. The League training, though part-time, is very intensive and takes two years to complete. All of them were married with young families. My daughter Vanessa also trained but completed her League training in England and also got her diploma in Physical Education in St. Mary's College in Twickenham.

1984 was the Golden Jubilee, we celebrated this with a big display in the UCD Sports complex.

Golden Jubilee 1984 - U.C.D.

By then I had three new teachers and the League started opening up new centres. By 1986 I knew we needed more teachers so started yet another course. This time I had seven students, again all handpicked from the classes. The age range was eighteen years to fifty years. At the time I was a little worried about the age range, I needn't have been. They all supported each other and I personally found them a very rewarding group to train. Two of them, Lidia and Nicola emigrated soon afterwards, Lidia is teaching League in London and is a Reader at Imperial College, London. Sylvia took over my evening classes and also teaches in Beechpark School, Stillorgan and is an Extend Tutor. Carol, Phyllis and Lorna have their own centres. Due to family commitments, Melinda is not teaching at present.

Golden Jubilee 1984 - U.C.D.

Sarah at League

Hazel - Movement is life !

At the end of each training year we always have a concentrated four days, a rest day and then two days of practical exams – performance and teaching. They already have had to pass their Anatomy, Physiology and First Aid exams.

In June 1988 they had their final week. On the Monday morning I woke with quite a severe pain in the pit of my stomach. I tried to ignore it all week, though it was steadily getting worse. The students had no idea that I had a problem; they had enough to cope with themselves. In the midst of all this, my grandson Adam had been born and I wanted to go to see him in the hospital. Friday evening our examiner, Pat Rowlandson arrived by boat and I met her. She was staying with me and over the years had become a very good friend so I admitted to her that I was feeling very ill. I had invited husbands, parents, etc. to our graduation evening on the Sunday and Tony Ward had agreed to present their diplomas. Of course it was at Invergarry and I was doing the catering. I look back with horror to that occasion but I didn't realise that the new teachers had noticed that I looked terrible and they thought they were responsible.

New teachers 1988
Back row: Melinda, Carol, Lorna, Lydia
Sitting: Sylvia, Nicola, Phyllis

My Illnesses

The following Monday I went to the doctor, he thought I had a bladder infection but very soon realised that I had a serious problem. After exhaustive tests, I understand patients are now anaesthetised for this, that was not the case then. I had an operation on 15th July 1988, with two surgeons present, as they were still not sure where the problem lay. I had third stage ovarian cancer – 'the silent killer' and I was given a maximum of five years to live. The following October Betty and I had planned to go to Australia to visit Truda and then on to New Caledonia in the South Pacific to where Vanessa had emigrated the previous year. The doctors told Gillian not to let me cancel my holiday; I think the reason was probably that they felt my survival prospects were very low. Adam was only a month old when I had the surgery, so he spent a lot of time in the hospital with Gillian visiting me.

The Gynaecologist who had operated on me and the Oncologist visited me the next day to give me the news and to tell me that I was to have nine months chemotherapy. When I asked them had I a chance they were very busy looking out the window or up at the ceiling and I got no reply, they just said they would arrange for me to have the necessary chemotherapy when I was in Australia.

Probably what stood to me so much was that prior to the cancer I had been very fit, also I don't think I ever accepted the thought of dying prematurely. I was 69 at that time but still considered that I had a lot to do and the overwhelming desire to make sure I did it. I was concerned about the Caravan Park, as I knew I could no longer run it. Fortunately I managed to sell it in September 1988.

Nowadays chemotherapy is less of a trauma than it was then. My oncologist did admit that they were able to give me a more severe treatment that could only be given to a very fit person. It was arranged for me to continue treatment in a hospital in Sydney, my friends managed to change that to a hospital near where they lived, which was 100 miles south of Sydney. I was always very ill after the chemotherapy, now they have pills to counteract this. I was particularly ill after my treatment in Australia, I gather it was because it was too quickly administered. We had arranged to go on a short cruise to the Barrier Reef, I was too ill to go but I persuaded Betty to go on her own. When I recovered I went to Vanessa but had to return to Australia for my next treatment, this time I was kept in hospital.

Betty with baby kangaroo - Australia 1988

Truda with Parakeets - Australia 1988

Truda's Cats - 1988

Vanessa is living in Noumea, which is the capital and only city of New Caledonia – a small island in the South Pacific. It has been a French Colony for about 150 years. The main languages are French and Melanesian. It is a long narrow island lying NW/SE and measures roughly 300 miles long and 30 miles wide. The high mountains and the nickel mining area divide the French settled region of the south from the less developed region of the north. The population of the island is over 204,000, the great majority of that is situated in Noumea. The time is 11 hours ahead of Greenwich Mean Time. Vanessa's pre-school is a short distance from the centre of Noumea and is very conveniently placed.

Regarding my illness, looking back it was all pretty traumatic but I always intended making a complete recovery, so no doubt, that was what kept me going. In April 1989 I was given the all clear but of course still had to have regular blood tests.

I have no idea who wrote the following but it aptly describes my philosophy and my outlook on life.

You Can If You Think You Can
(Author unknown)

If you think you are beaten, you are;
If you think you dare not, you don't;
If you'd like to win but think you can't,
It's pretty well sure you won't.
If you think you'll lose, you've lost;
For out in the world you'll find
Success begins with a person's will
It's all in the state of mind.

Full many a race is lost
Ere even a step is run,
And many a coward fails
Ere even his work's begun.
Think big and your deeds will grow;
Think small and you'll fall behind;
Think that you can and you will;
It's all in the state of mind.

If you think you're out-classed, you are;
You've got to think high to rise;
You've got to be sure of yourself before
You ever can win a prize.
Life's battles don't always go
To the stronger or faster man,
But soon or late the one who wins
Is the one who thinks he can.

For my 70th Birthday, Gillian and Dan organized a surprise party at their house. There were a number of friends past and present there.

My surprise 70th birthday party

With Dorothie at my 70th birthday party

Two and a half years later I was pretty sure I was in trouble again but nothing showed up in tests and I was diagnosed with diverticulitis. Frankly I didn't believe it but I wanted to visit Vanessa again. Betty and I got a great deal for a 'round the world trip'. This included a visit to Fiji where we met up with Vanessa who had travelled from New Caledonia with David who was only a baby. The Fijians are very friendly and they love children. David was in his element; he was so well looked after. I managed to enjoy some of it but deep down I was worried and feeling very poorly.

When I returned home I couldn't get an appointment with a specialist before Christmas. On Christmas Eve I was stuffing the turkey when I realised I could no longer cope with the pain. I ended up in St. Vincent's Hospital and spent Christmas there being treated for an abscess. To this day I cannot understand that with my history it was not realised immediately that I had cancer again. I asked could I see Mr. Hyland who had been present at my first surgery as then it was thought that I might have bowel cancer. As soon as he saw me he said he was pretty sure it was cancer.

I was just starting an Extend Course so I asked could I wait a couple of weeks. He suggested I rang him when I was ready which I did. He thought I might have to have a colostomy. After the operation he came to me as soon as I was conscious, told me he had done a laparotomy, that he had removed the omentum and that he was pretty certain it was cancer, but it was academic anyway as he had got it all away. I did not have to have any treatment, it was not secondary cancer so fourteen years on I am still here and still teaching!! I was considered a remarkable case!

During my chemotherapy I had consulted with a Doctor who was also a great believer in homeopathy. He advised some supplements that I should take and especially large doses of Vitamin C. Since my second surgery I eat a tremendous amount of fruit and vegetables and take daily certain vitamins that I know I lack in my diet. I am not fanatical about my diet and when I am on holiday I eat whatever is available. As I grow older I need less and feel better.

I don't want to tempt fate by saying my health is great or I may come down to earth with a bang! Having divested myself of Lindegay and the Caravan Park I was now freer to concentrate on the League and to enjoy my grandchildren.

With Sheila and Bobby at their Golden Wedding Anniversary

League Shows

By 1989 I was fifty years teaching, this was celebrated by a demonstration in the National Concert Hall in January 1990. This was such a success that I decided to repeat it almost two years later in aid of The Multiple Sclerosis Society of Ireland. To me it was also an act of faith as I had had my second bout of cancer and I felt I had something to prove.

My Golden Jubilee with family

Mandy Griffith presents bouquet to Prunella - 1990

Active Retired Group with Rhona - Concert Hall

A WOMAN OF REAL BEAUTY

NEVER than at Christmas does the League of Health mean more. This remarkable organisation has been celebrating the benefits of fitness and exercise long before Jane Fonda discovered plum puddings add inches.

Spearheading the Irish branch in recent times has been Isolde McCullagh who not only celebrated her sevenieth birthday this year but marked 50 unbroken years teaching in her Dun Laoghaire centre.

Three generations of women have flocked to her classes, new centres have been opened every year and since 1984, she has been the

central in the League's latest venture, bringing the benefits of exercise and movement to the elderly and the disabled.

Not only has Isolde also been an Irish swimming and diving champion, but taught ballroom dancing and ran her own knitwear company.

Eighteen months ago tragedy struck, however. She underwent surgery for advanced ovarian cancer, which was followed by nine months of chemotheraphy treatment. During this time, she not only started a new League course for teachers but travelled to New Caladonia to see a daughter.

She has never made a

secret of her illness in the hope it might give hope and encouragement to others in a similar situation. She now has a clean bill of health but in recognition and celebration of her achievement the League of Health plans a major public demonstration in the National Concert Hall, on Saturday, January 13, at 3 p.m.

Lined up is an afternoon of style, dance and fanfare with teachers, and pianists all taking part.

The League's motto is "movement is life". It has rarely meant more. Isolde was born in Dublin but went to London to train. World War Two drove her home,

where she trained under the equally legendary Kathleen O'Rourke, who founded the League in Dublin in 1934.

That's a long time ago. Emphasis throughout has been on good body coordination rather than physical over-exertion. Commercial need and greed has never interfered with the League's work. And Isolde McCullagh truly is a beautiful woman . . . in more ways than one.

Tickets for the afternoon in her honour are available from the NCH.

Newspaper Cutting 22/12/1989

At 72

THREE years ago, aged 69, Isolde McCullagh got a pain in the pit of her stomach and knew something was wrong.

"I'm so healthy that I never get aches and pains, so I knew there was a reason for this," she says.

It was ovarian cancer. "It's known as the silent killer, because sometimes it is well advanced before it's noticed. In my case I have such a healthy lifestyle that I recognised immediately that something was wrong."

She had major surgery followed by chemotherapy for nine months. "There were no side effects from therapy except nausea. I would allow myself a day or two to be sick and then get on with my life. I was too busy not to be well.

"Because of the extent of the pain, I was pretty sure it was cancer. The doctors confirmed the diagnosis after the operation and it wasn't really too much of a shock.

"What was a shock, though, was the fact that they couldn't get it all away, and for about 48 hours I wrote my obituary.

"But that didn't last long. I hadn't the slightest intention of dying. I decided I was not going to die. I've a lot of things left to do, and a lot to live for.

"I was never afraid, never shed a tear. This was something that happened to me and my response was to meet it head on. Ironically, I couldn't wait to get started on the chemotherapy and couldn't understand why the doctors wouldn't put me on it straight away.

"But when I went on it and realised how sick it can make some people, and I was one of the unlucky ones, I realised they felt they had to build me up first," she says.

Newspaper Cutting Evening Herald 13/11/1991

Isolde is principal of the League of Health of Ireland. She is responsible for a national organisation which has dozens of local classes operating each week, trains teachers in a rigorous two-year programme, offers courses to paramedicals, and founded Extend — a series of exercises for disabled or elderly people.

But in February this year, she suffered a double blow when cancer was diagnosed again, this time in her omentum, a protective flap hanging in front of the intestine which holds the lymph nodes.

"I thought I had it knocked and here it was again. But the good news this time was that I didn't need any chemotherapy.

"I'm philosophical about cancer. I tell people I've had cancer, past tense.

I do admit that sometimes when I read stories of well-known people who've been fighting cancer for years, write books about it, and are doing well, then suddenly you pick up the paper and they've died, well that shatters me for a while. But just for a while, then I'm positive all over again."

Second time round, she was operated on and within four weeks was back teaching. She's so well that she wants to take part in a major fitness demonstration this weekend. "I want to show that a diagnosis of cancer isn't the end."

The demonstration is a spectacular show of movement to music by the League of Health at the National Concert Hall on Saturday, November 16 at 3pm.

"The key is posture", says Isolde.

At 72, she is a good advertisement for her movement, supple in both body and mind. She is a fit, fulfilled, positive woman, mother and granny.

Newspaper Cutting Evening Herald 13/11/1991

Performing Aspects of Love - Concert Hall 1991. Lorna behind me.

Joan in Ribbon item - Concert Hall 1991

Keep Moving

At 77, Isolde McCullagh is as active as ever. A teacher with the League of Health since 1939, she still gives classes 6 days a week, as well as training other teachers for the League and its Extend programme which is aimed at older people. She believes in keeping busy and mobile, no matter what age you are. "There is a tendency for some of the medical profession to think that once people reach a certain age, they should accept certain ailments," says Isolde who believes that it is never too late to start getting active. She also points out that being retired does not mean you are old.

A former swimming champion – she won the Irish quarter mile in the early 1940s – Isolde has danced since she was 2 years of age and joined the League of Health in her late teens. The League was set up in Ireland in 1934 to give people of all ages exercise classes to music with special emphasis on posture.

Isolde was diagnosed as having advanced ovarian cancer 8 years ago, but was given the 'all clear' 3 years ago. "When you have a life-threatening disease, it would be easy to curl up and give up," says Isolde. "It is essential to keep moving."

Isolde advocates gentle, careful exercise rather than extreme forms of activity which can cause injuries if not taught properly. Regular, sensible exercise also helps fight depression. "Even your mental health is improved if you do something you enjoy," says Isolde. "When people who are busy all their lives retire, it is tempting to become a 'couch potato'; yet walking to the shops rather than using the car or using stairs rather than a lift is a more sensible lifestyle."

Newspaper Cutting Consumer Choice 1996

At a League refresher course in Largs in Scotland, I had met up with Diana Kropinska. She was Head League Teacher in Vancouver. As a student she had taught me Public Speaking. Subsequently she married a Polish pilot and they emigrated to Canada at the end of the 1939-45 war.

While on holiday in Canada, I contacted her. She invited me to one of her rehearsals for an item she was preparing for the 1980 Albert Hall Show. This turned out to be the most spectacular item I have ever seen at our Albert Hall Shows. Anyway our friendship blossomed and we found we had much in common in relation to the League work. We corresponded regularly and in 1983, she asked me to teach technique at her teacher's Summer Course.

I have a lot to thank Diana for, as it was she who made me feel I really had something special to offer the League as indeed I felt with her. She stayed with me for a few days in 1990 when over for one of the Albert Hall Shows.

With Diana

Irish Team performing in the Albert Hall 1990

Age 72

In 1990 I was asked to go to Auckland, New Zealand to help with training and to examine students. I had a hectic couple of weeks there and had wonderful hospitality with Colleen (a League member) and Max Hawthorne.

Since that time I have visited regularly to help train and to examine and was guest of honour at their Diamond Jubilee celebration. They also honoured me by making me their patron. On my last teaching visit I trained a number of them for Extend. I have a special relationship there – both with the League teachers and with their beautiful country. Sadly Max has since died and Colleen is now living in Christ Church in the South Island but we keep in touch.

With Colleen on her balcony in New Zealand

New Zealand teachers and new teachers just qualified 1993

New Zealand Diamond Jubilee 1995

A big added bonus is that it is only a two and a half hour flight from there to Vanessa and family in New Caledonia. Now I visit mainly to meet up with Vanessa and her boys; they travel to Auckland, which cuts a little off the long journey I have to make.

Catamaran Weekend New Caledonia

Vanessa's pets

Vanessa's School, Noumea, New Caledonia

Helping in Vanessa's Pre-School

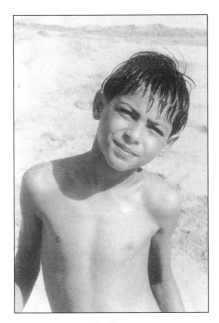

Mathew

David

Vanessa picking her banana crop

*There is a child sleeping in the bulim. Matthew is investigating.
New Caledonia*

Vanessa's School, Noumea, New Caledonia

With all the favourable publicity that the Concert Hall shows engendered I knew I needed to train more teachers. In 1992 training began. I gave it my all for two years; it was a huge challenge with so large a group of various ages and abilities. Thankfully they all did well and are now teaching mostly in new centres within a radius of 27 miles from the Centre of Dublin. Alison, Ethel, Hilary, Jennifer, Joan, Judy, Miriam, Valerie and Yvonne all now have their own centres. Miriam and Jennifer are also Extend Tutors; Jennifer is a Physiotherapist as well and has taken over Shirley's lectures. Ethel has taken over my Kill o' the Grange centre, she also choreographed our item at the Albert Hall in 2000. Lorna, from the previous group is choreographing our item for 2005. We have now 65 classes in 35 centres.

Pat presenting Miriam with her certificate

The graduation of this group coincided with the League's Diamond Jubilee in Ireland in 1994 and my fifty-five years of teaching. What started out to be a low-key celebration ended up in the Basketball Arena! Every seat was taken and the car park couldn't cope with the numbers. We had teams from the United Kingdom and representatives from New Zealand. It was a huge success but I took a long time to recover. My days of producing shows of this size are over and I doubt if anybody would be prepared to follow in my footsteps.

I was beginning to feel that my house was not my own and I seemed to spend my time moving furniture. I decided to find other venues for Extend Training, this was really necessary as most of the teachers tended to live on the south side of the city and we had many requests for teachers on the north side. Also Extend was beginning to spread to other towns and cities. By this time I had trained more tutors so was gradually withdrawing from active participation and trying to take a back seat as it were.

Basketball Arena 1994

Basketball Arena 1994
Hazel on left, Karen Williams on right. (Karen is now a
professional dancer with Andrew Lloyd Webber Company)

From the early days, since before I was a member, the League in Ireland has always taken part in the major celebrations in London. In 1939 a team came from Dublin to take part in a big demonstration in the Wembley Stadium.

Prunella conducting a rehearsal in Wembley Stadium for the
Empire Pageant performed later in the day by
the Women's League of Health and Beauty.

I was a student in London then but found it strange not being part of the Irish contingent. Of course all demonstrations ceased in the United Kingdom during the war years.

In recent years the shows are always held in the Royal Albert Hall. They occur every five years and we always have a team performing. They are really wonderful occasions. Teams come from all over the world, they only have a very short opportunity to rehearse at the venue, yet the whole show goes like clockwork and is a memorable experience for all those taking part.

By 1999 the League was 65 years in Ireland and I was 60 years teaching. The teachers organised a weekend in the Grand Hotel in Malahide. So many members came from the UK that we ended up with not enough room for the Irish. Still it was a very enjoyable weekend and a lot of work went in to organising it.

Malahide 1999 - My sixty years (me on right)

Both Prunella and Pat Rowlandson came over for the celebration, at this time Pat had been diagnosed with leukaemia, which she fought until she died in 2000. Pat had examined all the teachers I trained and had become a close friend. This is the hardest part of growing old, as slowly but surely one loses one's friends.

Isolde, Prunella, Pat and Elizabeth in Malahide

My Move to Bray

I had begun to feel that I should leave Invergarry and move into an apartment. It was not an easy decision, as it had been the family home for 48 years but it had seventeen rooms and I was there on my own. The final decision was made when Gillian and Dan told me that they had accepted an assignment with APSO to go to Namibia for 2 years, as Dan had been offered a lectureship in Special Education at a Teacher Training College.

For the last Christmas in Invergarry in 2000 they came home from Namibia and Vanessa, David and Mathew came from New Caledonia, Dallas was with us also, though as his marriage had broken up, his children were with their mother. I had found a lovely apartment near Bray with a view of the Dargle river and the Wicklow Hills.

New apartment

Gillian came home again to help me move which I did at the beginning of June 2001. Though the move was very traumatic I love my new home and settled down very quickly; having my West Highland dog – Pippa with me was a great help. While Gillian and Hazel were home, we had a lunch with friends to celebrate Betty's 90th Birthday. Betty was very interested in this book but sadly died just before it was printed.

Betty's 90th birthday with Gillian and Hazel - 2001

I had moved my Invergarry League classes to the Presbyterian Church Hall in York Road, Dun Laoghaire for the final Spring Term, as I wanted my members to get used to the change. They nearly had me in tears they were so upset that I was leaving Invergarry, I had taught there for about 45 years.

With Dan's mum, Mary, in my new sitting room

I planned to visit the family in Namibia in October/November, which gave me something to look forward to. As I had also been invited to attend the League's Golden Jubilee in South Africa, I was able to combine the two. Prunella had opened the first centre in South Africa 50 years ago and taught there for some time until her return to England.

The League term began, I had taught for two weeks and was preparing for my journey to Africa. On Monday 1st October 2001 I was in Bray, shopping; I had Pippa with me when I tripped crossing the road. Probably Pippa got a fright and ran forward, her lead was round my right wrist. Anyway I fell with such force that I broke my wrist, damaged my left knee, split my head open and broke my glasses. I was taken by ambulance to the nearest Accident and Emergency Department where I spent the usual five hours, an experience that many have to deal with and is not to be recommended! After X-rays it was confirmed that I had a Collis fracture. I overheard a discussion between two young doctors who examined my knee X-ray – "oh that's osteoporosis and arthritis, can't do anything with that!". When I was discharged my wrist had been put in temporary plaster, I was offered crutches, which I couldn't use because both arms were bruised, I couldn't walk because of the damaged knee. Dan's sister-in-law, Roseanne (my key holder) kindly picked me up and wheeled me to her car and took me to a friend's house. She had taken Pippa and she had me to stay as well for a couple of nights.

Thursday I had an appointment with the specialist who I was told would set my wrist. To my surprise he said he could do nothing, it would have a slight lump on it but would be fully functional. New plaster was put on and I continued to have a lot of pain, I queried this but to no avail. By then I was black and blue everywhere including two black eyes, which reminded me of a panda every time I looked in the mirror. Unfortunately I am very right handed and found it very difficult coping on my own. I would recommend everybody to train both hands in case of a similar mishap. I went on my trip to Africa, as can be read in the travel section, but managed to injure my leg there as well. However I did have the plaster off my arm in Windhoek, but it was still very painful and swollen.

Once home I needed to get attention for both my arm and my leg. While away I had been told by many in the medical profession that there was something seriously wrong with my hand and wrist. When visiting my local doctor to have my leg checked and to get suitable dressing for it, I showed her my hand. She immediately said that I had a problem and she wrote a letter to the 'specialist' I had to attend at the hospital. The said specialist did not like getting the letter and denied I had anything wrong. In his words "I was just not trying hard enough"!

Previous to seeing him I had talked to one of his assistants who told me I had a condition called Sympathetic Reflex Dystrophy. The only positive thing that came out of all this was that I could avail of physiotherapy at the hospital. I have nothing but praise for all the help I got in that department and was lucky to have a physiotherapist called Shirley, who did all she could with, I have to say, a pretty hopeless case.

After a few weeks treatment it was obvious that the reason I could not turn my hand was that the head of my ulna was sticking out. My elbow was permanently bent and I developed a frozen shoulder. I was really in a lot of pain and had a 100% useless hand and arm. I decided to get a second opinion, this resulted in Mr. John Varian of Blackrock Clinic operating on it in April 2002. From then on I never looked back. I attended Shirley for physiotherapy in Loughlinstown, who worked very hard with me. Between the two of us I now have a virtually fully functional hand and arm. What should have taken a few months to mend took nearly a year.

It was the first time that I had been seriously affected by age discrimination, there are some doctors that write you off once you reach a certain age, I have yet to discover what this age is!

Travel

Over the years Betty and I had many wonderful holidays. I never had the opportunity or the money to travel until I was in my sixties but made up for it since then. On one of our short cruises out of Athens, we visited Santorini. This island is an extinct volcano and the town is at the very highest point. The recognised way to reach it is by mule on a very narrow winding path. Betty, who was very heavy, was worried about a poor mule having to take her weight and had decided she would stay at sea level. As we were getting off the boat, I suddenly saw Betty being lifted high in the air by two brawny men and unceremoniously dumped on a mule. Her face was a study but it is an episode that always caused us amusement in the years to follow.

My first visit to Canada was in 1979, when Betty and I visited her brother and family in Ottawa and then went on to take the Rockies tour, finishing in Vancouver. A few years previously I had met a League teacher, Diana Kropinska in Largs, we immediately enjoyed each other's company, so when I reached Vancouver I contacted her.

From then on I used to break my journey to New Zealand and New Caledonia and always stayed with her en route. Sometimes I just made the journey direct to her, on one occasion it fitted in with Expo Vancouver and on another trip I cruised "Inside Alaska" which was a wonderful experience.

In latter years her health was deteriorating but she never gave into it. Sadly she lost the battle early this year (2003). I hadn't seen her for a few years but we corresponded regularly and I miss her greatly.

With Vanessa in Paris

In Egypt

Santorini 1975

*With the Captain and Betty on cruise
from Greek islands to North Africa*

Cruising inside Alaska

Skagway, Alaska

Camel Safari, Kenya

Cheetahs looking for prey, Kenya

Paragliding in Seychelles

Seychelles

During our trip to Fiji, Betty and I took a very basic cruise through the surrounding islands but we were well looked after and the food was excellent. I was the only woman to take part in an optional visit to an extraordinary island, which is a network of caves, all full of water. It has to be low tide even to get into them and the water is still very deep. The most hair-raising part was at the beginning. We were told to wear flippers, I didn't have any, but I was assured I would be alright as I was a strong swimmer. To enter the cave we were to dive down having taken a deep breath, swim under water for a few seconds and then we would be pulled through on the other side. But, of course, I managed to miss the entrance!! Having swum under water for a while I was beginning to wonder would I surface before my breathing gave out, (thank goodness for the League breathing!) when I was pulled out backwards. Some of the women and men who were wondering whether they had the courage to go at all made their decision to remain on 'terra firma' after seeing what happened to me!

Anyway I made it second time round and found myself in a pitch-black cave with all the Fijian guides making spooky noises and banging tins together. When our main guide lit his torch we found ourselves in this extraordinary shaped cave with quite a low roof. We all grabbed a raft and were pulled by the men through various caves again in the dark. I was unlucky enough to be on a corner so every now and again I bumped into rough rock. Fortunately I had my runners on, so I used my left foot at shoulder level as a buffer. We eventually came to a cave, which soared above us and was open to the sky and quite awe inspiring. After that we made our way back and had to repeat the dive under the rocks. A lot of the men cut their backs a bit but my swimsuit was high enough to save me. It was altogether a really scary episode. I am so pleased I went but if I got the chance I wouldn't do it again.

I have had many holidays in New Caledonia, usually staying about 5 weeks. Gillian and family travelled out to stay with Vanessa for 6 weeks in 1995. In 2002 I spent just a week with Vanessa in New Caledonia, then we had five weeks together in New Zealand, touring and staying in beautiful locations in the North Island. Vanessa hired a car, organised the trip and I just sat back and enjoyed it. I arrived still suffering from the aftermath of my fall but by the time I left I was a new woman!

With Vanessa on Isle des Pins 2000 - A wonderful weekend

Driving Creek Railway, Coromandel, New Zealand

With Vanessa and boys, New Zealand 2003

▶♦◀

Ten days after I broke my wrist, I left for Namibia, I had asked for assistance right through and I must say I was looked after by everybody and arrived in Windhoek, Namibia more or less intact. The family had been warned that I was not a pretty sight! It was great to be with them.

Namibia was formerly known as South West Africa, it was under German rule before the First World War. It was then controlled by South Africa until it gained independence in 1990, at that time it took English as its official language, although there are of course many local languages spoken by the different ethnic groups. Many people in the capital still speak German and a lot of Afrikaans is spoken amongst the white population, the latter making up 10% of the total population of 1.8m. It is about 13.5 times the size of Ireland and is a country of extremes and very unequal in that 10% of the population earn 65% of the income.

As Dan and Gillian's accommodation was a very basic bungalow on the college campus, they had arranged for me to stay at a very comfortable lodge (hotel). There was a swimming pool; I had a special plastic cover to put over the plaster so I was able to bathe. The first time I went in most of the staff stood around the pool fascinated. After a day or two they behaved quite normally towards me and indeed were more than kind.

With the Buckleys in Namibia

Gillian had been in Guiding from childhood and a unit leader for many years. She spent a lot of her time in Namibia building up the local Guide unit and really enjoyed this contact with the local children. I attended an enrolment ceremony, which took place under a Jacaranda tree in the grounds of a school for deaf and blind children. Hazel had done work experience in this school in the youngest class for deaf children.

Halfway through their assignment, Hazel felt she would prefer to return to Ireland and go to boarding school as she was due to go into 5th year, starting the two year course for her Leaving Certificate. The curriculum in Namibia would have been too different to allow her to come back into 6th year. She got a place in Wesley College and opted to remain as a boarder even when her family returned to

Dublin. Adam preferred to remain in Namibia with his parents and continue at Mweshipandeka High School. They felt that the most difficult subjects for him to catch up on when returning to school in Dublin would be Irish and Maths, so Dan worked with him on the Irish curriculum and Gillian did the Maths. She had to spend quite a lot of time preparing for these sessions as the Maths curriculum is very different from when she was in school!

I was very anxious to see as much as possible of the country while I was there. There was a good tarred road from Windhoek to the north going through Ongwediva where the family lived, but otherwise the roads were mainly gravel and I found long distances driving on these very painful for my arm. Because of this Gillian arranged a Fly Safari, which would take in a number of game parks, the coast, and of course the magnificent sand dunes for which Namibia is famous.

Dan left us to the local airport and we duly went to board the small plane. Gillian went up the steps ahead to hold a good seat for me. I didn't realise that the first step was so high; the 'rail' was a rope so gave with me. I fell backwards, could not grab the other rope with my right arm and ended up on the tarmac. Unfortunately as I fell my left shinbone came in contact with a sharp metal lever protruding under the bottom step, this resulted in a huge gash. The pilot and co-pilot administered first aid in a most professional manner. The temperature was way up in the thirties, I was more conscious of the heat of the tarmac than of the mess my leg was in. They wanted me to go to the local hospital, but Gillian was adamant that as the bleeding was stopped by the dressing, we should go to Windhoek (the capital) and go to the hospital there.

They radioed for a wheelchair to be at Windhoek when we arrived and for 'Medicare' to be there to take me to hospital. The ambulance was not there, so Roswitha, the friend of Gillian and Dan's who was meeting us, took me to hospital. I was there about three hours and had a wonderful young doctor looking after me. I had over thirty stitches in the wound and was warned that I would need a skin graft on my return to Dublin. It eventually healed naturally and I have only a very small scar left.

Every lodge we stayed in, I was looked after very well. My leg had to be dressed each day, sometimes by a manageress, other times by a courier or a driver. All lodges (hotels) have staff trained in first aid, so they all knew exactly what to do and the cleanliness and care was perfect. As distances are so vast they have to be prepared to deal with all sorts of incidents. Here I was in the "wilds of Africa" and quite honestly I couldn't have had better treatment.

Despite all this I really enjoyed the trip. It is such a vast country and yet the drivers took us over some pretty rough terrain and knew the best places to spot the animals. One trip especially stands out. Gillian and I were driven by a young man who obviously just loved

Namibia

Sand dunes in Namibia

Namibia

Enjoying the holiday despite appearances!

the animals. He had a special relationship with a white rhino and her offspring and always carried suitable food should he find them. Well we were very lucky. He stopped, got out of the jeep, gave them their treat and fussed over them for a while. He had been present when the calf had been born, so it grew up knowing him. We asked would it be safe for us to get out of the jeep, but he didn't recommend it!

Perhaps the other most memorable occasion was a picnic breakfast very early in the morning so that we could see the sun rising on the sand dunes. These are enormous and the colours have to be seen to be believed. We then flew to the coast and spent a couple of days where the temperature was cooled by the Atlantic breeze.

Our trip ended with a journey on the Desert Express back to Windhoek – Namibia's answer to the Orient Express. As it travels at a maximum speed of 20 k.p.h. there was plenty of time to view the countryside.

Once back in Windhoek I had to have an X-ray, then the plaster off my arm, a special wrist splint made, this was too painful to wear as the wrist and hand were so swollen. Then finally I had the stitches out of my leg. I was one week in Windhoek, five days of which I was being treated for either my arm or leg. We hired a car and Gillian drove me everywhere and the heat was intense.

Eventually I flew to Johannesburg where I was met by Betty O'Donoghue, who some years previously had travelled specially to Dublin to train with us as an Extend teacher. I stayed with her and her friend, Marilyn for a few days in Irene, near Pretoria. I visited some of Betty's Extend classes and was delighted to see how well they were going. We then travelled by car to Capetown for the League's Golden Jubilee. We took a day and a half and stopped at Karoo Park for one night. Karoo Park is the Khoi word for "dry thirst land". It is an ancient fossil-rich landscape with the largest variety of succulent plants found anywhere on earth. In 1689 Hendrik Oldenland sent a cutting to Europe, which was the forerunner of the international Geranium industry.

I stayed in the Victoria & Alfred Hotel, Cape Town, South Africa

Karoo Park, South Africa with Betty O'Donoghue and friend.

It was a wonderful trip and a great opportunity for me to see this wonderful country. The approach to Capetown is spectacular. I was so impressed with Marilyn's Audi car that I bought one the same when I was able to drive again.

I had booked a room in the Victoria and Alfred Hotel, quite the most luxurious I have ever been in and costing less than the most basic hotel in Ireland. Most of the UK team were staying there also, but I was one of the first to arrive. My cases were unpacked for me, my clothes pressed and even a notice in the foyer, saying "Welcome Mrs. McCullagh".

I was also looked after by the English team, most of whom had their husbands with them. It made what could have been a very difficult visit for me into an enjoyable one. I was in considerable pain and knew there was something really wrong with my arm. There was a programme of events organised by the League in South Africa including a demonstration and a luncheon and an evening of classes taught by various local and visiting teachers. Prunella Stack, of course was there as she had opened the centre fifty years ago.

Irish item at South African Golden Jubilee

Unfortunately I never got up Table Mountain, as there was too much wind for the cable car to operate. After the festivities were over I spent a few days with Mollie Warr, a League member of long standing who kindly looked after me until I left for home.

My return journey was not as pleasant, actually I really needed more help then, but as I had no longer a plaster on my arm I no longer looked disabled.

I returned to teaching in September 2002 and have cut it down to three classes a week in Dun Laoghaire. I still work with the League and Extend in an advisory capacity and am involved in all our fund raising activities.

The Family Today

Now I have more time for the family and can enjoy the grandchildren and my great-grandson.

My great grandson Paul

Despite being almost 85, I am still teaching three classes a week, still Principal of the League and Extend and I attend nearly every meeting.

I have three large balconies around my apartment with raised flower beds and one where I grow runner beans each year, so find I do more gardening than ever.

I swim at least once a week in Glenview Leisure Centre, often with Sheila, followed by ten mninutes in the Jacuzzi (pure bliss!) then a shower and usually followed by 10 – 12 minutes on the treadmill.

Socially I keep in touch with a group of friends with whom I was in Alexandra, I am also a member of the Trefoil Guild, which has monthly social gatherings for past Guides.

Paul, Sarah and Darren

Kenneth

Sarah

Paul

David

Mathew

Dan, Gillian, Hazel and Adam

With Vanessa

Hazel and Adam

I am a great believer in keeping up my interests, which I hope will help me to live to a ripe old age!

Gillian and family have settled back after their two years in Namibia, Dan is back in his previous job (he had been given a two year sabbatical) as Principal of a special school in Bray for children with a learning disability. Gillian is working as an Occupational Therapist with a school for children with behavioural difficulties. Hazel always enjoyed swimming and was in a club for a couple of years, but her main sport was skiing. For a number of years she was a member of the Irish Childrens' Race Squad, training and racing on dry slopes and on snow. She is now doing Social Science in UCD and has joined a number of the University sports clubs and societies. Adam is now in his transition year in Newpark Comprehensive School and appears to favour architecture or design for his future. He recently did work experience in the planning office of the local County Council and really enjoyed it.

Sarah works in her mother's business, her great love has always been horse riding and jumping. She now has her own home, where she lives with her partner, Darren and six year old son, Paul, an adored grandson for Dallas and great-grandson for me. Kenneth has another year in College to finish his business studies degree.

I decided to visit Vanessa again, immediately after Christmas 2002. Previously I had always stayed in Club Med as Vanessa was working all day and I had always gone to her in the autumn. She has made a great success of her own pre-school, which she built up on her own property, where she has her home, but she has had to work very hard to achieve this. Her boys – David and Mathew are both doing well at school. David's sport is sailing and Mathew's spare time is spent horse riding.

As Club Med has closed it seemed more sensible to visit at the height of the summer. I had a week with her, then I went ahead to New Zealand where she and the boys joined me for a wonderful 5 weeks. She hired a car and we saw a lot of the North Island and stayed at some beautiful beaches. I felt so much better after this holiday that I didn't take much persuading to return.

Travelling again to New Zealand in January 2004, allowed me to achieve a lifetime ambition, going up in an air balloon. This brings me back to the beginning where this book began.